The Wrightsville Beach Preservation Society would like to express its most sincere appreciation to the corporate sponsors whose generosity makes this book possible.

Bryant Real Estate

D & E Dodge, Jeep, Eagle

Nick Garrett/James Cooke Development

Blockade Runner Beach Resort

Oceanic Restaurant

All of the proceeds from this book go to the non-profit Wrightsville Beach Preservation Society and the Museum of History.

WRIGHTSVILLE BEACH
A Pictorial History

by **Greg Watkins**
and the Wrightsville Beach Preservation Society

THE
DONNING COMPANY
PUBLISHERS

The Donning Company/Publishers
184 Business Park Drive Suite 106
Virginia Beach, VA 23462

Steve Mull, *General Manager*
B. L. Walton, Jr., *Project Director*
Sally C. Wise, *Associate Editor*
Kevin M. Brown, *Senior Graphic Designer*
Monica F. Oglesby, *Imaging Artist*
Dawn V. Kofroth, *Assistant General Manager*
Tony Lillis, *Director of Marketing*
Teri S. Arnold, *Senior Marketing Coordinator*

Library of Congress Cataloging-in-Publication Data

Watkins, Greg, 1947–
        Wrightsville Beach: a pictorial history/by Greg Watkins & the
Wrightsville Beach Preservation Society.
                p.   cm.
        Includes index.
        ISBN 1–57864–009–1 (Hardcover: alk. paper)
        1. Wrightsville Beach (N.C.)—History—Pictorial works. I.
Wrightsville Beach Preservation Society. II. Title. F264.W9W37   1997
975.6'27—dc21   97-29720
                                                CIP

Printed in the United States of America

Contents

Dedication

In memory of Lucy Brewer, a founding sponsor of the Wrightsville Beach Preservation Society.

Acknowledgments

THIS BOOK, AS WITH ALL PRESERVATION EFFORTS, HAS BEEN A collaborative endeavor. Its purpose is to share our rich history and promote the preservation of our island.

∞First and foremost, I'd like to thank Bill Creasy for his dedication, inspiration, and untiring help on both the history and photographs.

∞In addition, the time and effort contributed by the following Preservation Society Volunteers were essential elements in jump-starting this book: Linda Caden, Penny Smith, Chris Oakley, and Ginger Kenny. Without their help, this book could not have been produced.

∞Beth Keane for her research expertise and assistance.

∞Editorial consultants: Anne Russell, Michelle Conger and Betty Bordeaux.

∞The archivists at the Lattimer House, New Hanover Public Library, and the Cape Fear Museum for their help in accessing resources.

∞Ronald Williams for donating the artwork.

∞To all those who donated their precious memories to the Wrightsville Beach Museum of History—which helped to make this publication so diverse and interesting.

This pictorial history book is not meant to be a definitive historical reference. Much of the information in this book was drawn from a variety of sources including *The Wilmington Morning Star*, *Land of the Golden River* by Lewis Philip Hall; *Historical Narrative 1841–1972 of Wrightsville Beach* by Rupert L. Benson and *Wrightsville Beach: Natures Nightmare or Sunny Sanctuary: History Honors Thesis* at the New Hanover County Library.

Early New Hanover County Map. *Courtesy of*

Thomas Shannon.

One

Our Beginnings:
Railroads to Trolleys and a Grand Style
(1853 to 1919)

WRIGHTSVILLE BEACH IS ONE OF A CHAIN OF islands off the east coast of North Carolina. Over the last one hundred fifty years, this small barrier island has grown from an isolated waterfront strand visited occasionally by sailors into one of the most popular tourist destinations on the eastern seaboard. In the process, Wrightsville Beach matured and justly earned its reputation as one of the friendliest places to live in the United States. The history of this dramatic transformation from secluded island to flourishing town fascinates not only the local resident, but anyone who visits the sparkling waters of Wrightsville Beach.

In 1853, seven yachtsmen led by Richard Bradley III formed the Carolina Yacht Club. This first structure on the beach was called the "Banks House" and is marked on an early map of New Hanover County. At that time, it was the only building on the beach and served as a gathering spot for gentlemen.

In 1874 the Wilmington and Coast Turnpike Company began taking stock subscriptions to raise funds to build a toll road to Wrightsville Sound. Construction began in June 1875 and was completed in January of 1876. The "Shell Road," as it was called, consisted of

The earliest known picture of the Carolina Yacht Club, the first structure on "The Banks," now known as Wrightsville Beach. **Courtesy of Emma W. MacMillan.**

The Shell Road covered a distance of approximately eight miles, and followed the path of present-day Wrightsville Avenue. *Courtesy of the New Hanover County Public Library, Bill Creasy Collection.*

Construction on the trestle began on March 12, 1888. *Circa 1910. Courtesy of the New Hanover County Public Library, Bill Creasy Collection.*

A toll gate for the old "Shell Road." *Courtesy of the Lower Cape Fear Historical Society.*

Left: **The train, and later the beach trolley, ran until 1940 between Wilmington and the beach.** *Circa 1910. Courtesy of the New Hanover County Public Library and Bill Creasy.*

a layer of straw with oyster shells on top. With time, wagon traffic crushed the shells and created a hard-packed road. In 1888 at the east end of the road, a train trestle was completed across the sound (later called the Intracoastal Waterway) to the Hammocks (later named Harbor Island). From this point a foot bridge led to Wrightsville Beach. That same year the Island Beach Hotel at the Hammocks opened with a restaurant on The Banks, which later became Ocean View Beach and finally Wrightsville Beach. Also constructed were two saltwater bath houses located in the center of the walkway over Banks Channel. In 1889 the Ocean View Railroad Company completed the trestle across Banks Channel to the beach, which quickly evolved into a fashionable recreation spot. Young, old, rich, and poor flocked to the beach, often from many miles away, to enjoy swimming, fishing, boating, dining and dancing. In that day of more moderate attire, women wore full bathing suits with wool stockings and booties covering their feet. The men swam in knee pants and sleeved shirts.

This Classy 0-4-2 tank engine was built by the Baldwin Locomotive Works for the Ocean View Railroad of Wrightsville Beach in 1889. She was brought to Wilmington on May 8, from Philadelphia, and put into service May 21. From Rails to Weeds, C. R. Kernan.

Moderate bathing attire was typical at Wrightsville Beach at the turn of the century. Courtesy of the Cape Fear Museum.

With easier access ensured, individual cottages, hotels, and other structures sprang up along the beach. In 1895, Michael J. Corbett, an Irish-American merchant from Wilmington, donated two ocean-front lots for a church which

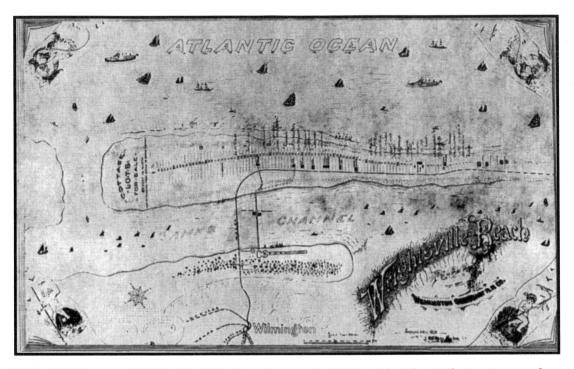

This 1897 map of Wrightsville Beach was published by the Wilmington and Seacoast Railroad. Note the inlet located where Ashville Street is today.
Courtesy of the Lower Cape Fear Historic Society.

The Seashore Hotel was one of the first large hotels built on Wrightsville Beach, opening in 1897. The Seashore promised plenty of seafood for fishermen, with all the modern conveniences. Over seventy feet wide and three hundred seventeen feet long, it contained one hundred eighty rooms with a pavilion connecting the hotel to the board-walk. Courtesy of the New Hanover County Public Library and Bill Creasy.

became known as St. Mary's-by-the-Sea. The small frame building seated about sixty parishioners and guests.

By 1897 more than fifty cottages and several hotels had been built. Among these were the splendid Seashore Hotel, Ocean View Hotel, Shelter of the Silver Cross (a home for sick children), the Atlantic Yacht Club, and of

course, the Carolina Yacht Club. Most of the cottages were not designed as permanent residences, but rather as fishing shacks, and later were built as vacation homes for the summer. This initial boom led to the official establishment of the town of Wrightsville Beach on March 6, 1899.

During the early twentieth century, most visitors to the beach took the train from downtown Wilmington and arrived at one of seven stations on the beach. After the line was electrified for trolley cars in 1902, for twenty-five cents visitors could purchase a round trip ticket to the beach and rent a bathing suit for the day. The ride on the beachcars, as they were called, from downtown Wilmington to the beach took about forty-five minutes.

With the arrival of lights, running water, and other modern conveniences in the early twentieth century, the pace of construction and settlement

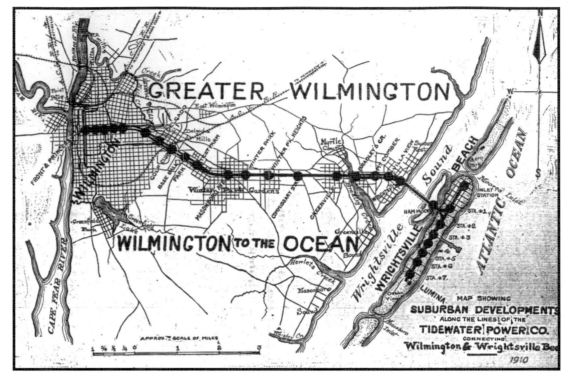

The trolley line ran eight miles to the beach, stopping at seven numbered stations on Wrightsville Beach. From the Bill Creasy Collection.

This ad appeared in the 1904 Wilmington Democrat *promoting the trolley line to the beach. From the Bill Creasy Collection.*

Beachcars, as they were called, were longer and had more seats than the regular trolley cars. The ride took about forty-five minutes. *From the Bill Creasy Collection.*

on the beach increased dramatically. Many beach homes were built in the vicinity of the trolley stops, stretching from the trolley trestle over Banks Channel to the south end. Most of these summer vacation houses were in a single row between the ocean and the trolley tracks. Near Station One and slightly to the north where the island was wider, more summer cottages were built on what was then referred to as the "northern extension." Ocean Avenue ran

When the beachcars arrived at Wrightsville, passengers could exit at one of seven stations. Pictured is Station One. Courtesy of the New Hanover County Public Library, Bill Creasy Collection.

In 1902 Tidewater Power Company purchased new railroad cars from the John Stevenson Company which ran on electricity. Here is the Wrightsville Sound power sub-station with the freight and passenger depot on the left. Circa 1919. From the Bill Creasy Collection.

parallel to and east of North Lumina Avenue. Over time, it was washed away by the Atlantic Ocean. Along with the numerous private cottages, large hotels and recreational centers were constructed. The Tarrymoore was built in 1905 and renamed the Oceanic in 1911.

The construction explosion continued throughout the early 1900s. By far the most memorable of these early structures was Lumina. Built in 1905 by Tidewater Power Company, Lumina, which literally means "beautiful palace of light," dominated the social scene on the beach for decades. A massive wooden Pavilion with three floors and many attractions, Lumina drew thousands of

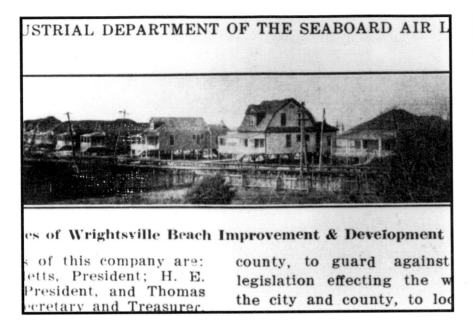

Ocean Avenue ran parallel to North Lumina Avenue and to the east, before it washed away. The view here is looking north up Ocean Avenue from Columbia Street to Charlotte Street. From the Bill Creasy Collection.

Just after 1900, this ad appeared in the Merchantile and Industrial Review of Wilmington and New Hanover County. It was issued by the Industrial Department of the Seaboard Air Line Railway, of Portsmouth, Va. The ad read, "One of the finest beaches on the Atlantic coast..there being two very fine hotels here that have a large and select patronage." In an effort to sell the houses, the ad went on, "A feature of this beach is the facilities afforded by the Wrightsville Beach Development Company in the matter of summer homes and cottages. This company completed during last season seventeen cottages, which it has fitted up in an elegant manner with electric lights, sewer, porcelain baths, running water and all modern improvements." Courtesy of the New Hanover County Public Library.

visitors each summer to dance "the rag" or "the castle walk" to such famous jazz musicians as Cab Calloway, Benny Goodman, Guy Lombardo, and "Satchmo," among others. Going through several periods of renovation and expansion, Lumina quickly became THE gathering place of the region. It boasted the first acoustically-designed stage and ballroom in the southeast, and according to many old timers, was also the finest. A 1912 Chamber of Commerce publication stated, "at Lumina, all classes meet on the same footing without friction or disorder of any kind, to the mutual benefit and comfort of everyone." It went on to say, "Wrightsville Beach is replete with amusements, sports and pleasures. Aside from the dancing in Lumina and the Hotels, and the

The Tarrymoore Hotel was opened in 1905 by W. J. Moore of Charlotte. It offered one hundred seventy-five rooms, a bowling alley, billiard room, saloons, card parlors, and excellent food. The opening of large hotels such as the Tarrymore spurred the development of the beach in the early 20th century. From the Bill Creasy collection.

Lumina Pavilion, constructed in 1905, dominated the social scene at Wrightsville Beach for decades. Courtesy of the New Hanover County Public Library, Brimley Collection.

Lumina, which literally meant "beautiful palace of light," could be seen for miles at night. *Courtesy of the Cape Fear Museum.*

Right: **A cozy Corner at Lumina provided a place both to see and be seen.** *Courtesy of the New Hanover County Public Library, Bill Creasy Collection.*

Visitors flocked to Wrightsville Beach each July 4th, one of the busiest days of the summer. In 1910, over five thousand people visited Lumina on Independence Day.
Courtesy of the Cape Fear Museum, New Hanover County Public Library, Bill Creasy Collection.

ever-popular surf bathing, there are numerous contests and tournaments. These were in the form of yacht races, canoe races in the ocean surf and on the sound, foot-races, and nearly every kind of athletic sports."

While Lumina was growing, the grand style associated with it developed in other places on the beach around the same time. In early 1906, members of the Hanover Seaside Club decided to build a clubhouse at Ocean View Beach. Property on the southern extension a few blocks north of Lumina was purchased for $500 on May 16 from Aaron A. Nathan and his wife Janette Nathan. The club's membership consisted primarily of immigrants from the Province of Hannover in Germany. The purpose of the club was to provide a place to socialize and preserve language and customs, and it still exists today.

A 1912 Chamber ad read: "Wrightsville Beach is replete with amusements, sports and pleasures." Foot races, sack races, greased pole climbing, and beauty contests were regular events. Top and bottom left photo courtesy of the New Hanover County Public Library, L. T. Moore Collection; Bottom right photo courtesy of the New Hanover County Public Library, Bill Creasy Collection.

Courtesy of the Cape Fear Museum.

In August 1906, beach costumes were still somewhat conservative. Courtesy of the North Carolina State Archives.

This 1906 photo shows the brand new Hanover Seaside Club at Wrightsville Beach. Club subscribers were largely immigrants from the Province of Hannover in Germany, interested in providing a place to socialize and preserve their language and customs. Courtesy of the Hanover Seaside Club.

By 1907 Wrightsville Beach was an established resort with many families from North Carolina and the surrounding states coming to spend the entire summer at the beach. It was at this time that the Rev. Richard Hogue, rector of St. James Episcopal Church and Dr. John M. Wells, pastor of the First Presbyterian Church, saw the need for more than just a neighborhood Sunday School. Since the majority of the full time summer residents were from these two congregations, funds were contributed and a small building was constructed on the sound side of South Lumina Avenue near Station Two. It is

Programme

CONCERT AND SOUVENIR DANCE
GIVEN BY

The Celebrated Lumina Orchestra
AT
LUMINA

Tuesday Night, September 7th, 1909.

...CONCERT...

1. March—"Tannhauser" . . . . . Wagner
2. Grand Selection—"Bohemian Girl" . . Balfe
3. Baritone Solo—"My Rosary" . . . Nevin
   Mr. Frank Banks.
4. Excerpts from—"Carmen" . . . . Bizet
5. Descriptive Fantasia—"A Day With a Circus" . J. B. Lampe
   SYNOPSIS—The Band—Drum Corps—Bagpipes—The Plantation—Singers—Banjos—The Orchestrone—Chimes—The Colored Band—The Caliope—The Spielers. PART II—Rush for Tickets—Passing Through the Animal Tent—Rush for Seats—The International March—Trapeze Performance—Elephant's Dance—Indian War Dance—Bare Back Riders—The Chariot Race—Grand Finale.

DANCE PROGRAM.

1. Two Step—"The White Wash Man" . . Schwartz
2. Waltz—"Blue Danube" . . . . . Strauss
3. Two Step—"Gee! I Wish had a Girl" . . LeRoy
4. Barn Dance—"Kerry Mills"
5. Waltz—"When I Marry You" . . . Gumble
6. Two Step—"Mandy Lane" . . . . McKenna
7. Waltz—"The Girl Question" . . Jos. E. Howard
8. Barn Dance—"S. R. Henry's"
9. Two Step—"I Love My Wife, But Oh You Kid" . Von Tilzer
10. Waltz—"Home Sweet Home"

LUMINA CONCERTS
JNO. F. KNEISEL, Conductor.
CONCERT ORCHESTRA OF 16 PIECES

Program, Sunday, July 24th, 1910

AFTERNOON—4:00 O'clock

1. Medley—"Whats the matter with Father?" Remicks
2. Overture—"Orpeus" Offenbach
3. "Narcissus" Nevin
4. Selection—"Time, Place and the Girl" Jos. E. Howard

PART II

5. Medley Selection—"Remick's Hits No. 6" Arr. Lampe
6. Grand Selection—"Maritana" Wallace
7. "Polish Dance" Scharwenka
8. Final—"Put on your Old Grey Bonnet" Van Alstyne

NIGHT—8:30 O'clock

1. "Tannhauser March" R. Wagner
2. Selection—"The Chocalate Soldier" Strauss
3. Audante from Symphonie No. 6 Hadyn
4. Selection—"Faust" Gonoud

PART II.

5. Characterestic—"Baby Parade" Pryor
6. String Quartette—"Berceuse" Bohm
   Kneisel String Quartette
7. Overture—"Poet and Peasant" Von Suppe
8. Rag—"Pickled Beets" Ed. Kuhn

Typical programs of the day. *Courtesy of the Wrightsville Beach Museum and Betty Bordeaux.*

reported that Thomas H. Wright, Sr., suggested the name, "The Little Chapel on the Boardwalk."

In the 1910's, even during World War I, Wrightsville Beach continued to blossom socially and economically. The huge Lumina Pavilion, with its programs, concerts, and competitions continued to draw large crowds. On a much smaller scale, the Onondaga Tea Room, which was part of the Oceanic Hotel complex, began operating on Banks Channel just north of the trolley trestle. The steel pier opened at the Seashore Hotel in 1910, the first pier in southeastern North Carolina, and was over seven hundred feet long. In 1911 the Tarrymore Hotel became the Oceanic Hotel and improvements were made. More ever-popular boarding houses and Inns were completed as the island grew, and "North End Extension" was developed as far North as Augusta Street by 1910.

Initially an inaccessible though beautiful strand along the coast, Wrightsville had changed dramatically during its first seventy years of existence. By the 1920's Wrightsville Beach had overcome violent storms, devastating fires, and the Great War to firmly establish itself as a major coastal destination, not only in North Carolina, but throughout the East Coast.

This 1912 photo shows sailboats tied to the trolley trestle across Banks Channel. The building in the right corner is the Onondaga Tea Room, established in the same year. From the Bill Creasy collection.

Left: The Tarrymoore changed its name to the Oceanic Hotel in 1911. Note the beach car in front of the hotel. Courtesy of the Lower Cape Fear Historic Society.

Bathing Beauties by the Seashore Pier

The Seashore Hotel sat on the same portion of the beach that is currently occupied by the Blockade Runner. In 1910 the Steel Pier opened at the Seashore Hotel. This was the first pier in southeastern North Carolina and extended over seven hundred feet and included a well-lighted pavilion at the end with a large observation deck. From September 1920 to January 1921 violent storms destroyed the pier. *Courtesy of the New Hanover County Public Library, Bill Creasy Collection.*

Spectators flock to a biplane after it landed at Wrightsville Beach in 1911. *Courtesy of the New Hanover Public Library, Lucy Marguerite Hatcher Collection.*

The Harbor Island Auditorium was built by the Tidewater Power Company and opened in 1916 with a seating capacity of over two thousand. From a 1931 Tidewater Power Company promotional brochure, courtesy of the Wrightville Beach Museum of History.

Created in 1914 by covering marsh land with dredged material, "tent city," located just south of Lumina, consisted of twenty-six structures of varying size and offered cheaper living quarters at the beach. *Courtesy of the New Hanover County Public Library, Bill Creasy Collection.*

Right: **In 1916 the fishing was very good. These contest winners ate well for some time. Note the weights of the catches at the bottom, each about forty pounds.** *Brochure courtesy of the Wrightsville Beach Museum.*

New Hanover Fishing Club

Season 1916

Fishing Contest and Casting Tournament

OFFICERS

T. G. EMPIE, *President*
J. R. HANBY, *Vice-President*
H. R. AIKIN, *Secretary*
A. J. MITCHELL, *Treasurer*

CONTEST COMMITTEE

W. J. SWAILS, *Chairman*

J. L. GALLOWAY   B. H. BURRISS   G. W. ANDERSON
A. H. CREASY   B. T. HOPKINS   J. T. NEWMAN

MEMBERSHIP NOW OVER TWO HUNDRED

*Typical ads in the 1910's and 20's. From
the Bill Creasy Collection and the Wrightsville
Beach Museum.*

*A baby parade at Lumina. Prizes were given for the best decorated baby
carriage. Pictured here are Martha and Vergé Beall. Photo circa 1919. From the
Bill Creasy Collection.*

Above: **A beach car arrives at Seagate Station on the way to the beach. J. T. Baird, a former employee of the Consolidated Railway, Light, and Power Co., remembers that "during the twenties and thirties the beach cars were twice as long as the city street cars, each had a seating capacity of sixty-eight people, but could easily carry a hundred and often did."**

Left: **Horsing around for the camera are John Batson in front (later operated the Esso station) and Charles Roberts behind him (started C. S. Roberts Groceries). The smaller beach car in the rear ran to the north end of Wrightsville, near Augusta Street. From the mid-twenties.** Courtesy of John Batson.

Two

The Roaring Twenties and the Not So Depressing Thirties

THE FIRST STOP ON THE BEACH WAS STATION One, where beach car travelers departed to a modest covered station with open sides. On the west side of the tracks, a two-story wooden structure was erected in 1925 and called the Channel View Hotel. The ground floor of the hotel was divided, half for the dining area, and half for Pop Gray's soda shop. "Pop Gray," known to thousands of young people for two decades, acquired his nickname from a character in a newspaper strip called "Harold Teen," in which Pop Gray operated a soda shop called the "Sugar Bowl." Wrightsville Beach's Pop Gray was a duplicate of this character, thin with sparse hair and an iron gray mustache. Pop Gray's was a favorite meeting place for young and old. One of the many kids to hang around Pop Gray's was a fifteen year-old named Punch Pullen. Punch recalls, "Money was not so plentiful, and we needed a job to make enough to attend the Lumina dances. I took a job with the Ideal Laundry and when guests arrived on the trolley, I would be on the alert at Pop Gray's soda shop to see where they would be staying. The next day I would be out pushing my laundry cart to their homes to see if they needed laundry services." On the front of the cart read; "Calling Punch Pullen." One day Punch saw a cute girl with her large

"Pop" Gray's Soda Shop was located at Station One and occupied half of the ground floor at the Channel View Hotel.

The inside of Pop Gray's Soda Shop. Circa mid-twenties. Courtesy of John Batson.

Right: **Punch ("Who's that?") Pullen at age fifteen in 1925, provided laundry services to summer visitors. In the background is the Ocean Inn (near Station One).** *Courtesy of Punch Pullen.*

family moving in. The next day, Punch, true to form, knocked on their door to see if he could get their laundry business. Punch remembers, "She answered the door and promised me her laundry if I would get her a cute date for the dance." He replied, "I'm not cute, but I'll take you to the dance if you promise me your laundry." Punch got the laundry and a summer romance.

Punch Pullen also recalls the day a gentleman came into Pop Gray's who had never seen the ocean before. He asked for a Coke bottle to take a little bit back home, and a cap for the top. Pop Gray is reported to have said, "Sure, but don't put the cap on too tight or it will blow off at high tide!"

On the east side of the tracks in a junction of the boardwalks was Bud Werkauser's stand, Pop Gray's competition. The small, wood frame, open-air structure was painted a battle-ship gray. Here cold drinks, newspapers, and souvenirs were sold. Station One became a bedlam of sound and activity upon each beach car's arrival. J. T. Baird remembers, "During the twenties and the thirties the beach cars were twice as long as the city street cars.... each car had a seating capacity of sixty-eight people, but they could easily carry a hundred and often did."

White-coated young Negro porters, each pulling a small four-wheel wagon, vied with each other for the baggage of the tourists. During the three months of the summer season, thousands of people from all over the north and south came to this island. Friday and Saturday nights were the big nights of the week, and from 7:30 to 9:30 in the evening the boardwalks at Station One would be crowded. From the northern extension hotels, boarding houses, and private cottages came the beach colonist, tourist, and excursionist, all converging on Station One.

The "Snow Birds" at this time made their appearance. Composed of a group of Negro boys dressed in white duck pants, white shirts, and black bow ties, the Birds entertained the crowds at Station One. One Snowbird would hum through a piece of tissue paper wrapped around a comb and play the melody. A jugman supplied the bass, an ordinary tin funnel became either a

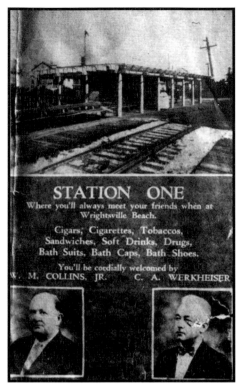

STATION ONE
Where you'll always meet your friends when at Wrightsville Beach.

Cigars, Cigarettes, Tobaccos, Sandwiches, Soft Drinks, Drugs, Bath Suits, Bath Caps, Bath Shoes.

You'll be cordially welcomed by

W. M. COLLINS, JR.   C. A. WERKHEISER

On the east side of the tracks in a junction of the boardwalks, at Station One, was Bud Werkheiser's Stand. This building later became the fine brick building of Newell's Shopping Center. From a 1928 newspaper ad, courtesy of the Wrightsville Beach Museum of History.

Mrs. Werkheiser and Pop Gray.
Courtesy of John Batson.

On an adjacent corner from Station One stood the huge, impressive Oceanic Hotel, which ran from North Lumina Avenue to the ocean. **Courtesy of the Cape Fear Museum.**

Right: **The full moon swim was extremely popular during the early twentieth century. With the summer heat, many locals and visitors elected to "bathe" after six in the evening to enjoy the cooler temperatures.** **Courtesy of Bill Creasy.**

mellow saxophone or a "hot" trumpet and another youth had thimbles on his fingers that ran over the metal ridges of a washboard, beating out the rhythm of real syncopation. At intervals each member of the band put aside his instrument for a moment to cut a buck and wing, the crowd went wild with enthusiasm and coins showered down on the swinging band. Eventually a talent scout in the crowd heard the group and lured it away to New York City.

On an adjacent corner from Station One stood the huge, impressive Oceanic Hotel, which ran from Lumina Avenue to the ocean. Guests in fine evening attire could be seen meandering about before and after dinner on the vast porches and promenades. Dinner music wafting out into the night could be heard for blocks away.

On January 16, 1920, prohibition became law with the passing of the Volstead Act. It was highly resented by many Americans, making lawbreakers out of otherwise law-abiding citizens. Although Wrightsville Beach was no stranger to prohibition, having been "dry" since 1909, even here citizens indulged in some home brew. In those days when proper etiquette was the norm at Lumina, folks at intermission could be seen on the boardwalk away from the bright lights, pouring from half gallon jugs into cups and hoisting them with the old "here's mud in your eye" salute.

Also in 1920, on the nearby mainland, another important development was taking place which would affect many Wrightsville Beach residents for years to come. Dr. Sidbury and his nursing staff opened Baby's Hospital on June 6th. The original wooden structure was destroyed by fire in 1927 and replaced with a brick building which still stands on the original site.

Dr. Sidbury and his nursing staff at Babies Hospital which opened June 6, 1920. This building was destroyed by fire in 1927 and replaced with a beautiful brick structure at the corner of Wrightsville Avenue and Summer Rest Road. Courtesy of the Cape Fear Museum.

During the thirty-odd years of entertaining the public, and in spite of the great crowds attending the dances at Lumina, no disturbances of any consequence occurred. This was primarily due to the vigilance of the floor manager, W. B. 'Tuc' Savage, a six-foot-five-inch, two hundred fifty pound, sun-burned muscle of a man. Very few men, and no boys, EVER put up an argument with him.

In the twenties, festivities took place on both sides of Lumina. On the ocean, contests, competitions, pageants, and movies; on the sound side, boat races, sliding boards, and easier swimming were enjoyed. The Garber-Davis orchestra opened the summer season of 1923 at Lumina under the personal direction of Jan Garber, who went on to become one of the "Big Bands" of the

The wide staircase and platform which crossed over the trolley tracks provided easy access to the activities on the sound side of Lumina. Courtesy of Bill Creasy.

The calmer waters of Banks Channel were an attraction for many of the visitors to Lumina. Courtesy of Bill Creasy.

Sporting the waters of Banks Channel could be either high tech or low tech, depending on your style. Note the steering wheels in the power boats, and the Oceanic Hotel beyond the canoe. The lady in the canoe is Edith Creasy.
Courtesy of Bill Creasy and the Lower Cape Fear Historic Society.

E. L. Hinton advertises in the late twenties the renewed Seashore Hotel featuring the "highest standards of American Plan service." Courtesy of the Wrightsville Beach Museum.

1936–1942 era. The orchestra played for dances and Sunday concerts every night at Lumina until the season closed on Labor Day. The following year, Weidemeyer and his orchestra opened the summer season with Al Gold as director.

Besides playing for dances each week night at Lumina Pavilion, the Weidemeyer orchestra also furnished the nightly dinner music at the Oceanic Hotel, free of charge. Weidemeyer and his Orchestra were young men, mostly college graduates, handsomely dressed in mohair tuxedos. Hanging from the ballroom ceiling at Lumina was a huge globe completely covered with tiny mirrors, and when the beautiful strains of a waltz, such as "The Sweetheart of Sigma Chi," emerged from the orchestra, the lights were lowered and a spotlight was thrown on the revolving ball. Then every young man took his best girl to dance on the huge and shiny dance floor.

This group is having fun sailing in the Channel.
Photo from the Tidewater Power Company promotional brochure dated 1930. Courtesy of the Wrightsville Beach Museum.

Lifeguards from the late twenties. The guard on the right is Bunny Hines.
Courtesy of John Batson.

The Batson Cottage and original Kitty Cottage as viewed from Banks Channel, just south of the trolley trestle.
Photo from the mid-twenties. Courtesy of John Batson.

Across Moore's Inlet at the northern end of Wrightsville Beach, the unspoiled shore and dunes were known as Shell Island. In 1923, C. B. Parmele and Thomas Wright, president and vice-president of Home Realty Company, purchased Shell Island and developed it into an exclusive Negro resort. Electric lights, sewers, water works, a large pavilion, bath houses, restaurants, cold drink stands, piers, boardwalks, and private cottages were installed.

Transportation to Shell Island was provided by the Tidewater Power Company by way of a spur track from the main line to the northern end of Harbor Island. At this point, waiting rooms were built and the Stone Towing Company of Wilmington provided a ferry to transport passengers across the inlet to the resort.

Weidemeyer and his orchestra were young men, mostly college graduates, dressed handsomely in their mohair tuxedos, and extremely popular. They played each week night for dances at Lumina, and evening dinner music at the Oceanic Hotel. Courtesy of Bill Creasy.

Advertisement from 1923: "Be There, Big, Little, Old and Young-You'll Have a Jolly Good Time." From a 1923 Tidewater Power Company rate schedule and advertisement, Bill Creasy Collection.

This early twenties postcard shows the Octagonal Tea Room between the wings of the Oceanic Hotel on the ocean side, which locals referred to as the "Round House." Courtesy of Bill Creasy.

Shell Island was advertised in 1923 as *The National Negro Playground.* **Courtesy of the Lower Cape Fear Historic Society.**

Bottom Left and Above: **In 1925 Charlie S. Roberts opened his grocery store at the corner of Sweeny and North Lumina and lived in the adjacent apartment.** *Portrait photo courtesy of Eva Cross. Store photo courtesy of the New Hanover County Public Library, Bill Creasy Collection.*

Lewis Williams recalls that when he was a young lad on summer Sundays at 8 a.m, he and his brother Lawrence and their mother, Lillian Pierce Williams, would arrive at 13th and Ann Streets in downtown Wilmington and board a "special" beach car bound for sun and surf at Shell Island. At the big powerhouse station on Wrightsville Sound, they crossed a narrow trestle to the Harbor Island Causeway. Just before reaching the trestle at Banks Channel, the beach cars turned sharply to the left and ran to the northern extension of Harbor Island. At the end of the spur, beachgoers awaited the arrival of the small ferry to transport them across Moore's Inlet to Shell Island. The ferry was long and light in color with seats on one side, open above the gunwales, and covered by a canvas top. A concession stand near the center of the boat sold popcorn, cotton candy, and colored pinwheels which hummed in the breeze. Although Lewis was afraid of the water, he was always excited to go to the beach. While the other boys made a bee-line for the breakers, Lewis was content to build sand castles and listen to the music from Shell Island Pavilion. "There was never any trouble on those trips to Shell Island. Everyone was pleasant and orderly. It was good clean fun, a time I will always remember," Williams recalls.

The road to Wrightsville Beach was a beautiful ride in the twenties. Shown here is a section of Airlie Road. Courtesy of the New Hanover County Public Library.

Visitors from fifty cities in ten states, and from a number of foreign countries came to "Shell Island, the National Negro Playground." But after a series of fires plagued the public buildings, the island was abandoned and the structures left to deteriorate.

Shortly after the A. E. Fitkin Company bought out the Tidewater Power Company, Fred A. Matthis, now representing the Wilmington-Wrightsville Beach Causeway Company, announced that an agreement had been reached to build a causeway from Wrightsville Sound Station to Harbor Island. When completed, the causeway would run parallel and south of the trestle of the electric car line to Harbor Island, where free parking spaces for several thousand automobiles would be provided free of charge.

*Above: **At 4 o'clock on June 10, 1926, a motorcade of seven hundred automobiles moved across an area which had long been monopolized by steam trains and trolley cars.** Courtesy of Bill Creasy.*

In a Hurry Use the Causeway

Buy ticket book for automobile at the causeway, making a charge of approximately five cents each way for automobiles.

Wilmington-Wrightsville Beach Causeway Company

In the late twenties, ads enticed the travelers and signs showed the way for motorists to use the causeway to access the beach. *Lower left courtesy of Bill Creasy. Transfer ticket courtesy of Leila Wootten Miller. Lower right courtesy of New Hanover County Public Library.*

The plans also included a walkway across Banks Channel from Harbor Island to the beach for the convenience of motorists. At 4 p.m. on June 10, 1926, ribbons were cut across the western entrance to the Wrightsville Beach Causeway and a motorcade of seven hundred automobiles moved across an area which had long been monopolized by steam trains and electric trolley cars.

On the morning of April 5, 1928, a large sperm whale washed up on Wrightsville Beach. Its skeleton now resides in the North Carolina State Museum of Natural History. Courtesy of Bill Creasy.

On the morning of April 5th, 1928, M. M. Riley, Jr. a year round resident of Wrightsville Beach, rose early to take his before-breakfast walk. Stepping into the bright sunshine on his front porch, he stood gazing in complete amazement at the enormous form which was practically lying in his front yard. He was looking at a large sperm whale measuring 54 feet 2 inches in length and 33 feet in girth. The tail was 14 feet wide and the lower jaw 10 feet long, with an estimated weight of fifty tons. Within hours news of this phenomenon reached Wilmington. Soon cars were bumper to bumper across the newly-constructed causeway to Harbor Island, filled with curiosity seekers trying to catch a glimpse of the huge mammal.

The private lawn and flower garden of the Riley's cottage became "public property" as strangers tramped back and forth across the yard. More than 50,000 people from a half dozen states visited the site.

Wrightsville Beach authorities called the State Museum of Natural History and Resources in Raleigh and offered the whale, and it was accepted with the understanding that the whale be removed to Topsail Beach, an uninhabited island fifteen miles north of Wrightsville Beach, to decompose.

Live Oak Drive in 1926. Courtesy of the Wrightsville Beach Museum, Tidewater Power Co. brochure.

In 1928 Oliver T. Wallace began advertising for the development of Harbor Island. Courtesy of the Wrightsville Beach Museum.

Aerial view of Harbor Island. Note the Auditorium on the right Circa 1930. Courtesy of New Hanover County Public Library, Robert M. Fales Collection.

The Stone Towing Company of Wilmington was hired to remove the whale, nicknamed "Trouble" by locals due to the stench, from the beach. It took two tugs to return the carcass to the sea, then float it to Topsail. In September 1928, Harry T. Davis, the museum director, returned to Topsail Beach to determine whether the buried bones of the whale had lost enough oil to permit their shipment to the State Museum. The carcass was then shipped by railroad to Raleigh.

Development of Harbor Island went into full swing in 1928 with the Shore Acres Company. At the time of the stock market crash in October 1929, the backbone of the economy in Wilmington and the surrounding area was the General Offices of the Atlantic Coast Line Railroad system which provided employment to thousands of people. The dollars of the tourists and the people of New Hanover County were

Left: **This baby parade took place at Station One (note beach trolley car on left) in the late twenties.** *Courtesy of the New Hanover County Public Library, L. T. Moore Collection.*

Cars ran every half hour to the beach on the big weekends, as advertised in this 1929 Independence Day program. *Courtesy of Bill Creasy.*

The Carolina Aces played Lumina Pavilion in 1928, 1929, and 1930. Frank R. King, a member of the orchestra, donated this photo to the Preservation Society.

After this storm in the late twenties, not much was left of Ocean Avenue (it was to the east and ran parallel to North Lumina Avenue). Courtesy of the New Hanover County Public Library, L. T. Moore Collection.

Bathing beauties line up to strike a pose for the gallery. Courtesy of the New Hanover County Public Library, L. T. Moore Collection.

Beachcar number 57 crosses the Bradley Creek trestle. From the Bill Creasy Collection.

The Coast Guard practices a life-saving drill on the beach in the twenties. Courtesy of the New Hanover County Public Library, L. T. Moore Collection.

important to the businessmen of Wrightsville Beach, who made every effort to make their property as attractive as possible. One incentive offered to entice the public to continue to use the beach railway was the combination ticket. It entitled the purchaser to board a beach car anywhere along the line, ride to the resort, be admitted to Lumina to dance or watch a silent movie, then ride back to the city near midnight, all for sixty cents. Hundreds of couples from the city went to the weekend dances, which were the most popular. Even during the Depression, life at Wrightsville Beach with all its events, competitions,

WRIGHTSVILLE
BEACH

a real ocean resort near
WILMINGTON, N. C.

Season 1930

Train Service · Schedules · Round Trip Fares

Tide Water Power Co.
Atlantic Coast Line

Left and below photos: In 1930 the Tidewater Power Company produced this service and rate schedule. It was a terrific promotional brochure for Wrightsville Beach. **Courtesy of the Wrightsville Beach Museum.**

Top Photo Above: **The dance floor at Lumina, the "Summer Social Capitol of the Southeast."**

Bottom Photo Above: **Pomander Walk, one of the more charming choices in accommodations, opened in 1929 directly adjacent to Lumina on the Sound side.**

Above: **This "C" Class sailing competition was held in Banks Channel circa 1930. Note Harbor Island in the background.** *Courtesy of the Wrightsville Beach Museum, Marion Myers Haubner Collection.*

The Kitty Cottage, said to have derived its name from the kitty of the poker games that were frequently held there. Shown here is the rebuilt cottage in its new location near Station Two. Courtesy of Bill Creasy.

Right: **The Tar Heelia Inn (on the left) was built in 1910. It was the northernmost cottage on the island for decades, occupying lot 54 - the last lot on "North End Extension." The small house to the right is the E. F. Peschau cottage. Elizabeth Dock Bordeaux is on the left with an unidentified friend.** *Circa 1926, photo courtesy of the Wrightsville Beach Museum, Betty Bordeaux collection.*

and celebrations continued in full swing.

Visitors to the beach had a wide selection of accommodations. Adjacent to Lumina were the quaint Pomander Walk apartments. Located midway between Lumina and the children's playground and bordering the Lumina Pier Boardwalk, the Pomander Walk Apartments were built around a well kept grassy quadrangle. There were sixteen three-room suites and four four-room apartments, with green roofs and awnings. During the twenties, thirties, and forties the boarding house was one of the mainstays for visitors to Wrightsville Beach. Among these were large cottages like the Kitty Cottage, Tar Heelia Inn, Ocean Inn, Parsley Cottage, and Edgewater Inn.

Others were huge buildings that rivaled the magnificent hotels of that era. The Hanover Inn was one such popular destination. Built circa 1900 by a Mr. Wright, it was later sold to Captain Sherman and then in 1946 to James A. Burgess. It had forty bedrooms, a kitchen and dining room, and plenty of piazza space to capture the ocean breeze.

One of Harbor Island's best known and largest landmarks was frequently referred to as the "Pink Club." Perched on Banks Channel just north of the trolley line and causeway, this beautiful structure was used during World War II as a USO club and later as the beginning of the Wrightsville United Methodist Church. J. Harris Ligon purchased the cottage, and the house

HANOVER INN
ONE BLOCK FROM BUS STOP
OCEAN FRONT
WRIGHTSVILLE BEACH, N. C.

Above: **The Hanover Inn was one of the larger inns at Wrightsville Beach, consisting of forty rooms. It was destroyed in 1954 by Hurricane Hazel.** *Courtesy of Jeanette Greiner.*

View south from Station One; note the Ocean Inn and Hanover Inn signs. Dual tracks were in place at Station One and at Lumina, giving beachcars the opportunity to pass one another. *Vintage postcard courtesy of Bill Creasy.*

The clean, clear waters and wide beaches are touted in a Tidewater Train schedule and rate pamphlet. It also says, "Wrightsville Beach enjoys a clientele of knowable, worthwhile folks...No objectionable features or people thrive at this Beach."

Right: These 1930 ads promoted the opening of the season at Lumina starting June 2nd. They featured "Jelly" Leftwich and the Duke University orchestra. Courtesy of Bill Creasy.

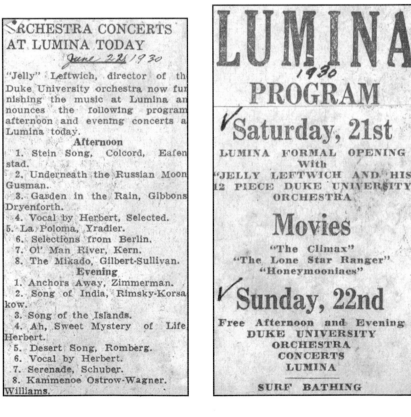

ORCHESTRA CONCERTS AT LUMINA TODAY

June 22, 1930

"Jelly" Leftwich, director of the Duke University orchestra now furnishing the music at Lumina announces the following program afternoon and evening concerts at Lumina today.

Afternoon
1. Stein Song, Colcord, Eafenstad.
2. Underneath the Russian Moon Gusman.
3. Garden in the Rain, Gibbons Dryenforth.
4. Vocal by Herbert, Selected.
5. La Poloma, Yradier.
6. Selections from Berlin.
7. Ol' Man River, Kern.
8. The Mikado, Gilbert-Sullivan.

Evening
1. Anchors Away, Zimmerman.
2. Song of India, Rimsky-Korsakow.
3. Song of the Islands.
4. Ah, Sweet Mystery of Life Herbert.
5. Desert Song, Romberg.
6. Vocal by Herbert.
7. Serenade, Schuber.
8. Kammenoe Ostrow-Wagner. Williams.

LUMINA
1930
PROGRAM
✓ **Saturday, 21st**
LUMINA FORMAL OPENING
With
"JELLY LEFTWICH AND HIS 12 PIECE DUKE UNIVERSITY ORCHESTRA"

Movies
"The Climax"
"The Lone Star Ranger"
"Honeymooniacs"

✓ **Sunday, 22nd**
Free Afternoon and Evening
DUKE UNIVERSITY
ORCHESTRA
CONCERTS
LUMINA

SURF BATHING

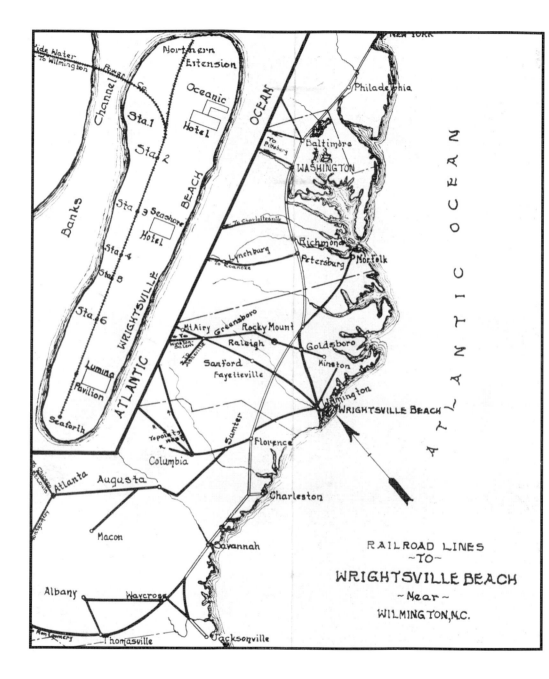

RAILROAD LINES
~ TO ~
WRIGHTSVILLE BEACH
~ Near ~
WILMINGTON, N.C.

The walkway across Banks Channel viewed from Harbor Island. *Circa 1930, courtesy of Bill Creasy.*

Left: **The railroad lines to Wrightsville Beach.** *Tidewater Power Company map circa 1930, courtesy of the Wrightsville Beach Museum.*

These packed beachcars are on their way to Wrightsville Beach, crossing the Bradley Creek trestle. Courtesy of the New Hanover County Public Library and Bill Creasy.

Right: **Aerial view of the north end of Wrightsville Beach circa 1931. The majority of development stops at Augusta Street, with the inlet in the general vicinity of where Johnnie Mercer's Pier is today.** Courtesy of the North Carolina State Archives.

remained in the family until 1996, when it was sold to a developer who demolished this classic landmark and replaced it with several homes.

The Harbor Island Casino, which was adjacent to the "Pink Club," opened on the night of July 1, 1933. The feature act was Dr. Katz and his "Kittens." The Casino, overlooking Banks Channel, closed in 1937. Also built in the early thirties was the replacement cottage for the Wilmington Light Infantry (WLI) Club on Channel Avenue. The club's first cottage was located elsewhere on the beach and was destroyed by fire. In those days it was used as a private bottle club by ex-military men. The WLI Club is still in its location on Channel Avenue and is used now as a family weekend retreat for descendants of the Wilmington Light Infantry.

January 28, 1934, Edmund Rogers was strolling along the beach when he noticed smoke coming from the Kitty Cottage, a large summer boarding house operated by Mrs. J. A. Snyder. Vergé Beall Emory recalls hearing the terrible sound of the fire bell, which meant something was ablaze. As was typical in the thirties, everyone, even children, volunteered to help with the bucket brigades. But it was of no use; the fire spread quickly and enveloped the Parsley boarding house along with several other private cottages. The Wilmington Fire Department responded, and a fire truck was loaded on a Tidewater Power Company flat car and brought to the beach by rail. When it was unloaded it immediately got stuck in the deep sand and was useless. When the wind shifted and increased to gale force, burning embers were carried to the shingled roof of the Oceanic Hotel. The hotel quickly became an inferno, its flames spreading northward from Station One to more than one hundred twenty-five cottages and structures. Vergé recalls leaving her home on Wrightsville Beach for the safety of Harbor Island, then looking across Banks Channel and watching her house burn. Betty Bordeaux recalls her great-aunt, Lillian Williams Huggins, describing the fire, "Everyone was in

The "Pink Club," built in 1930 as an exclusive beach club for notable Wilmingtonians, was sold in 1941 to the Salvation Army, which opened it as a United Service Organization (USO) Club, to serve the large influx of service men and women to the area. It was later used by the United Methodist Church, then sold to J. Harris and Ollie Ligon. In 1996 it was sold to a developer and torn down. Photo by Greg Watkins.

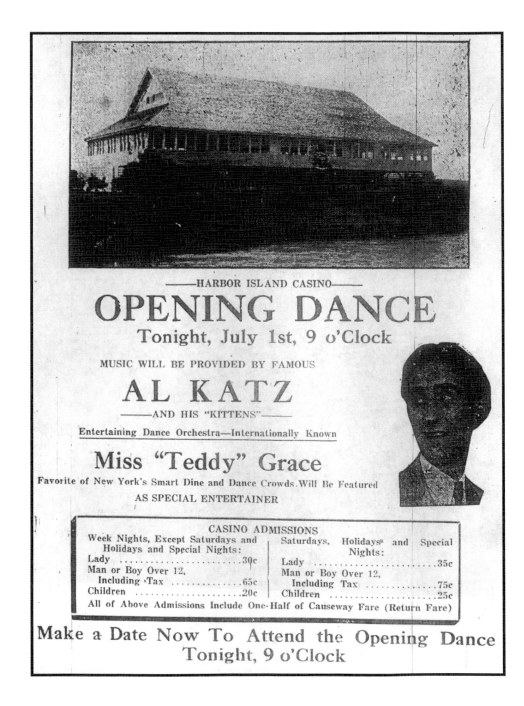

—HARBOR ISLAND CASINO—

OPENING DANCE

Tonight, July 1st, 9 o'Clock

MUSIC WILL BE PROVIDED BY FAMOUS

AL KATZ

——AND HIS "KITTENS"——

Entertaining Dance Orchestra—Internationally Known

Miss "Teddy" Grace

Favorite of New York's Smart Dine and Dance Crowds. Will Be Featured

AS SPECIAL ENTERTAINER

CASINO ADMISSIONS	
Week Nights, Except Saturdays and Holidays and Special Nights:	Saturdays, Holidays and Special Nights:
Lady 30c	Lady 35c
Man or Boy Over 12, Including Tax 65c	Man or Boy Over 12, Including Tax 75c
Children 20c	Children 25c
All of Above Admissions Include One-Half of Causeway Fare (Return Fare)	

Make a Date Now To Attend the Opening Dance Tonight, 9 o'Clock

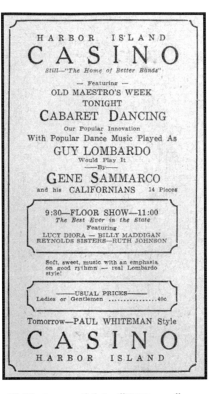

HARBOR ISLAND

CASINO

Still—"The Home of Better Bands"

— Featuring —

OLD MAESTRO'S WEEK

TONIGHT

CABARET DANCING

Our Popular Innovation

With Popular Dance Music Played As

GUY LOMBARDO

Would Play It

—By—

GENE SAMMARCO

and his CALIFORNIANS   14 Pieces

9:30—FLOOR SHOW—11:00
The Best Ever in the State
Featuring
LUCY DIORA — BILLY MADDIGAN
REYNOLDS SISTERS—RUTH JOHNSON

Soft, sweet, music with an emphasis
on good rythmn — real Lombardo
style!

——USUAL PRICES——
Ladies or Gentlemen 40c

Tomorrow—PAUL WHITEMAN Style

CASINO

HARBOR   ISLAND

Al Katz and his "Kittens" were the feature attraction on opening night at the Harbor Island Casino in 1933. The Casino was built by the Seashore Amusement Company next to the exclusive Harbor Island Club (the "Pink Club"). Inside the Casino the orchestra shell was on the west side of the pavilion and around the dance floor were comfortable opera chairs for spectators. The dance floor was one hundred eight feet long and sixty-four feet wide. Many famous orchestras came for one night engagements.
Courtesy of Bill Creasy.

Below: **The Wilmington Light Infantry Club house was built at this site on Channel Avenue in the early thirties as a replacement for the first clubhouse which was destroyed by fire.** *Photo by Greg Watkins.*

The Babies Hospital faces the sound, and was rebuilt beautifully with brick after the original building burned. *From the Tidewater rate schedule, courtesy of the Wrightsville Beach Museum.*

A sea plane visits the Frying Pan Yacht Club (located at the end of Sweeny Street). *Circa 1930. Courtesy of Bill Creasy.*

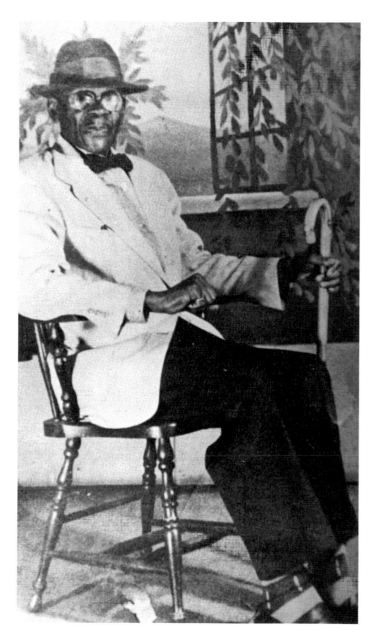

Left: **"Watermelon Joe" Howard was a popular vendor at Wrightsville Beach. He would sing as he hawked his wares.** *Courtesy of Anne Russell.*

Atlantic Coast Line Train Service and Excursions to Wilmington, N. C., Wrightsville Beach

SUMMER SEASON 1933

Excursions

ONE-CENT-PER-MILE between all points in Southeast, including St. Louis, Evansville, Louisville, Cincinnati, Birmingham, Nashville, Chattanooga, Atlanta, Washington, Richmond, etc., and Wilmington, N. C.

July 1, 2, 3   Limited Lv. Wilmington returning: July 9
Aug. 4, 5   "   "   "   "   Aug. 12
Sept. 1, 2, 3   "   "   "   "   Sept. 9

Also excursions from certain points in Alabama, Georgia, Tennessee and Mississippi to Wilmington and Wrightsville Beach on following dates:

June 9, 10; July 14, 15; Aug. 11, 12. Sample fares from—

	5 Day Limit	10 Day Limit
Birmingham, Ala.	$ 9.00	$11.00
Atlanta, Ga.	6.00	8.00
Meridian, Miss.	11.50	13.50
Chattanooga, Tenn.	9.00	11.00
Nashville, Tenn.	13.50	16.50

Summer excursion tickets with limit of 75 days are sold to Wrightsville Beach daily from all points in Southeast at one fare plus 1-9 for the round-trip. Season limit summer excursion tickets, with limit October 31, on sale to Wrightsville Beach daily throughout summer.

Bargain Week-End excursions are operated every Friday, Saturday and Sunday from Rocky Mount, Goldsboro, Sanford and Fayetteville, N. C., and Marion, S. C., and intermediate points to Wilmington, limited to midnight following Monday.

The Tide Water Power Company will sell from their Transportation Office, Second Floor, Front and Princess Sts., round-trip tickets via their electric line to Wrightsville Beach for 25c (50% reduction) for each adult holder of A. C. L. Bargain Week-End excursion ticket (15c for children's ticket).

Train Schedules

NEW YORK, PHILADELPHIA, BALTIMORE, WASHINGTON, RICHMOND AND WILMINGTON

NORFOLK, ROCKY MOUNT, ASHEVILLE, GREENSBORO, RALEIGH AND WILMINGTON

ATLANTA, AUGUSTA, COLUMBIA AND WILMINGTON

MT. AIRY, GREENSBORO, FAYETTEVILLE AND WILMINGTON

ATLANTIC COAST LINE

A COOL PLACE TO LIVE

Wrightsville Beach was a "Cool Place to Live" and you could get there for one-cent-per-mile on the Atlantic Coast Line Train. *Courtesy of the Wrightsville Beach Museum of History.*

View looking north (top photo) and south (below) from the top of the water tank by Station Four with the Carolina Yacht Club in the foreground. From the Bill Creasy Collection.

One of the rare photos of the great fire in 1934. The blaze destroyed over one hundred cottages and the Oceanic Hotel. Courtesy of The Morning Star.

a panic trying to save furnishings and personal belongings; they were even throwing telephones out the windows." As Lillian Huggins watched the inferno creep toward her cottage on the southwest corner of North Lumina Avenue and Augusta Street, the wind direction changed, and the cottage was spared the flames. The fire stopped at Augusta Street and many homes to the south were gone. Only six cottages to the north still remained. The Tar Heelia Inn's roof caught fire in three places, but fortunately it did not spread to the rest of the house. The fire was a devastating blow to the beach, but reconstruction soon began and Wrightsville started to get back on its feet again.

On October 6, 1935 the State completed the road extension over Banks Channel to Wrightsville Beach. The extension brought to fruition what the state had wanted for a long time, a system of roads from the mountains to the sea. Now you could reach Wrightsville Beach by car without walking across Banks Channel, so the need for the famous "beach cars" lessened considerably.

A beach car approaches Wrightsville Beach in June 1938. In the distance is the roof of the "Pink Club" on the left, and the Casino on the right. From left to right, identifiable boats are: No. 1-Captain Wells, No. 3-Valhalla, and No. 4-Althea B. Courtesy of Charles Riesz.

Left: Aerial view after the fire. Note the Oceanic Hotel is gone, as are many of the cottages, including all of those to the east of Ocean Avenue. Also note the newly-constructed Waynick Blvd. and the road extension over Banks Channel. Courtesy of the North Carolina State Archives.

The Ocean Terrace opened in 1937. The Anchor Inn is the building on the soundside, which had a rooftop beer garden and dance floor. Courtesy of Bill Creasy.

During the late twenties, Mr. & Mrs. Lester Newell moved to the beach and took over operation of the concession stand owned by the Tidewater Power Company at Station One. Later, Newell bought the stand from the Tidewater Power Company, but in those early years the stand was simply an open-sided stand with fold-up sides.

Deane Lomax Crowell remembers walking to Newell's from her home on the north end of Harbor Island. That first afternoon in August 1939, "We walked over the wooden bridge linking Harbor Island with Station One. We were on our way to Newell's for a milkshake made by hand by Mrs. Newell, the mother of the owner."

The Seashore Hotel opened the season of 1931 with the music of the Carolina Tar Babies, a university orchestra. At Lumina, "Jelly" Leftwich and his Duke University Orchestra would begin their fourth season in 1933.

1938 and 1939 tickets for the Wilmington Seacoast R.R. View is from the walkover at Lumina, looking north. The bath house is seen on the right. Courtesy of Bill Creasy.

ATLANTIC VIEW PIER

Atlantic View Fishing Pier was the predecessor to Johnnie Mercer's Pier. *Photo from the late thirties. Courtesy of Bill Creasy.*

Atlantic View Pier on a crowded afternoon. *Courtesy of the New Hanover County Public Library, Bill Creasy Collection.*

The Glen, a seasonal favorite since the late thirties. It is still located at the south end of the beach and managed by Naomi Yopp, whose mother built it in 1939. *Photo by Greg Watkins.*

By the spring of 1935, the really big name bands came to Lumina. Now the people of southeastern North Carolina could see the famous musicians and vocalists who in former years had only been names and sounds. Thousands of people came to Lumina to dance to Paul Whitman, Guy Lombardo, Jimmy Dorsey, Tommy Dorsey, Sammy Kay, Vincent Lopiz, Hal Kemp, Ted Weems, Stan Kenton, Kay Kyser, and many others.

Paul T. Marshburn of Wilmington, owner of the C & W Booking Agency, brought to Wilmington not only the big bands of the late thirties and early forties but celebrities for the Azalea Festivals. Marshburn will tell you that during World War II when there were thousands of workers at the shipyard, he booked a name band at either Lumina or the Harbor Island Casino almost every weekend. Known to many as Paul T., he was a plump, jovial man who began his career in the musical world during the early twenties when he played saxophone with the New Hanover High School orchestra.

The festivities at Wrightsville in the thirties were not confined to Lumina Pavilion. Water sports continued their popularity with power boat racing and sailing on both sides of the island. Development of residential cottages continued to grow, and among the new buildings in 1939 was a three-story wood frame structure on the corner of South Lumina Avenue and Nathan Avenue called the Glen. Mrs. Esther Naomi Yopp drew up the plans for the building and hired a contractor to build it. Her daughter, also named Esther Naomi Yopp, inherited the business from her mother in 1972. The inn still fills each summer with repeats, and some new guests who have heard from their friends about the friendly atmosphere. Today the Glen still has the same rocking chairs on the porch, the same neon sign, and the same furniture in four of the twenty-four rooms that it had when it was built in 1939.

Women bathers at Wrightsville Beach around the turn of the century. Courtesy of Bill Creasy.

Southern view from Oceanic Hotel of Wrightsville Beach. Note the Seashore Hotel and steel pier in the background. Circa 1919. From the Bill Creasy Collection.

The Seashore Hotel with its seven hundred foot steel pier and two gazebos, one with an observation deck, was a big attraction. Post card circa 1918. From the Bill Creasy Collection.

The Tarrymoore Hotel stood across from Station One, and in 1911 changed its name to the Oceanic Hotel. *Postcard from the* *Bill Creasy Collection.*

The Harbor Island Auditorium was located at the corner of the trolley line (later Causeway Drive) and Banks Channel (Live Oak Drive), built in 1916. *From the Bill Creasy Collection.*

Station Four on the trolley line was the Carolina Yacht Club. *Postcard from the Bill Creasy Collection.*

The Oceanic Hotel was the center of social activity in the Station One area until it burned in the great fire of 1934. Courtesy of Bill Creasy.

Left: **The Lumina ballroom was an attraction for many throughout the eastern seaboard for a generation.** *From the Bill Creasy Collection.*

Speed boat races were popular in the calm waters of Banks Channel. The young lad with the tan shirt and white pants is John W. Creasy. The twins at water's edge with striped shirts are the Holland boys. *Postcard dates from the forties, from the Bill Creasy Collection.*

Left: **Town municipal dock at the corner of Causeway Drive and Waynick Blvd.** *Circa late forties. Courtesy of Bill Creasy.*

Soldiers dancing during World War II. Courtesy of the Wrightsville Beach Museum.

Three

World War II, Development, and Booming into the 60's

THE ADVENT OF WORLD WAR II SIGNIFICANTLY affected Wrightsville Beach. The coming of the shipbuilding industry in Wilmington and the troops at nearby Camp Davis put housing pressures on Wrightsville Beach to change from a place of summer cottages to one of permanent homes. Modest cottages were winterized and expanded, and larger boarding houses were filled with military personnel and their families. Residents tell tales of driving with dimmed lights at night, and seeing horseback beach patrols on lookout for German submarines.

Deane Lomax Crowell's memories of the war years at Wrightsville Beach include:

"The early morning waits for a school bus for New Hanover High School in the days of double-daylight-saving time to conserve electricity for the war effort.

Watching my father, an air-raid warden, walk up Channel Drive in his gleaming white hat in full moonlight, while on the horizon incendiary bombs flamed in the oil slicks.

The four of us giggling when our mother in her long nightgown stepped into the bathtub filled with water (in case houses caught fire during those frightening nights).

Standing on the dunes near Newell's in the sunshine amid the waving sea oats and watching young sailors come ashore in rubber dinghies.

Soldiers with Wrightsville Beach girls, from left to right: May Daniel Carr Fox, Barbara Allen Darlen, Doris Caldwell Tienken. Courtesy of the Wrightsville Beach Museum of History.

These photos were in a Camp Davis brochure, which was published in the forties. Courtesy of the Wrightsville Beach Museum.

The booming shipbuilding industry in Wilmington, and the influx of soldiers from Camp Davis turned Wrightsville Beach into a year-round community. Courtesy of the New Hanover County Public Library.

They walked by.... near us.... most blond and blue-eyed with stubble on their chins, looking very tired and even more frightened. Some seabirds, gulls, pelicans, and loons, were beginning to die from the oil which blackened the beach for a time. We found the bird bodies for weeks, tried to bury each one, and grieved for the useless slaughter."

In 1940, the tracks for the beachcars that once took people to Lumina were removed and the steel sold to the Japanese. Some natives claimed it was used to make bullets to shoot American soldiers. During World War II, the once-brilliant lights of Lumina were blacked for fear of attracting German submarines which supposedly lurked off shore.

Even during the war, residents had to endure the wrath of Mother Nature. Eva Cross (who today runs Roberts Grocery) tells the story of a summer day in the late forties when she and her husband were managing the Tar Heelia Inn. She had spent most of the morning preparing supper for those who were staying at the boarding house. When her husband arrived home, he said he heard on the car radio that a bad storm was coming, and they all

Mira Mar Terrace advertised Wrightsville beach as North Carolina's most popular resort in this early forties post card. It was adjacent to Lumina, on the site of what later became Crystal Pier. The charming couple in the center are Jane Fielden and Leamon Rogers, whose father owned a grocery store on the beach. Courtesy of the Wrightsville Beach Museum.

Johnny Mercer, left, his wife Wanda, and Vance Horton with an unidentified employee, operated the counter at Johnny Mercer's Pier in 1941. Courtesy of Bill Creasy.

Atlantic View Pier (Johnny Mercer's) in 1941. Note the small pier house. Courtesy of Bill Creasy.

During the war, many military families rented rooms in the boarding houses. In this 1944 photo, a mother (and daughter) whose husband was a doctor at Camp Davis rented a room in the Tar Heelia Inn. The little girl on the steps with her kitten is *Sandra Cross Pendergraft.* Courtesy of the Preservation Society, Eva Cross Collection.

Claude E. Sanders (Eva Cross' father) in 1944. Courtesy of the Preservation Society, Eva Cross Collection.

Left: **Parties and dancing remained in full swing into World War II. Shown here are Jimmy and Ailene King.** *Courtesy of the Wrightsville Beach Museum, Gene Raines Collection.*

A dance night at Lumina is enjoyed by Doris Ulmer, Ailene King, Franklin Ulmer, and Billy Ulmer. *Courtesy of the Preservation Society, Billy Ulmer collection.*

Left: **An entertainer treats the queen and her court to a laugh at Lumina.** *Courtesy of the Preservation Society, Billy Ulmer Collection.*

A day at the beach in the forties. *Courtesy of the New Hanover County Public Library.*

Jeanette and Jimmy Burgess enjoy a summer day at Wrightsville Beach. She is held by Louise Jackson, with Banks Channel in the background, at 124 South Lumina Avenue. Jeanette and Jim Greiner, together with Jan and John (Jeanette's brother) Burgess, donated their vintage cottage to the Wrightsville Beach Preservation Society in 1995 to be relocated, restored, and opened as the Town Museum. Circa 1941, courtesy of Jeanette Greiner.

Youngsters enjoy the view from Harbor Island, looking towards Wrightsville Beach. Courtesy of the Preservation Society, Billy Ulmer Collection.

Wrightsville Beach police department on Waynick Blvd in the early forties. The Town employed two policemen during the winter months and three during the summer. Courtesy of the New Hanover County Public Library.

Right: **The fire department in the early forties boasted a modern five hundred gallon triple combination Mack fire engine and an auxiliary five hundred gallon Packard pumper.** *Courtesy of the New Hanover County Public Library.*

needed to leave immediately. Eva Cross had a kitchen full of guests and hot food and would have no part of that, so they all sat down to eat. She went upstairs for a moment and glanced out the window, and saw the Atlantic ocean coming up Augusta Street towards the house. She ran down the stairs and informed everyone she had reconsidered, and they all needed to leave right away.

The B & M Esso Station, operated by John Batson and Charlie Mills from 1946 to 1981 on Harbor Island. *Courtesy of John Batson.*

Jim Burns fills up his Buick roadster at the B & M gas station. *Courtesy of John Batson.*

The social scene at Wrightsville Beach continued to thrive during the early forties. On April 15, 1941, an informal meeting was held at the home of Charles Parmele to discuss plans for a proposed Beach Club. Those present at the meeting were Emily Parmele, Billy Corbett, Mary Green, Mike Brown, Platt Davis, Lewis Hinton, and Fannie Crow. In July 1941 a newspaper headline read, "Opening of Surf Club Attracts Interest of Local Socialites." With two hundred members, the Surf Club began, and is still at its original location at 1 Mallard Street. The article went on, "Slated to become a popular gathering place for members of local society, the Surf Club will offer tempting menus for various parties."

The Crest began showing motion pictures at the beach on Nov. 24, 1946. Constructed of brick at 18 North Lumina Avenue, it had a seating

Right: **Elaine Cartier Creasy at age eighteen in front of the Seashore Hotel.** **This 1948 photo is from the Bill Creasy Collection.**

The municipal dock at Wynn Plaza circa 1946. Just behind the sign is the Nautilus Restaurant, which later became the laundromat. Courtesy of the North Carolina State Archives.

The Bankhead Neptune Restaurant open in 1946. Courtesy of the New Hanover County Public Library, Rupert L. Benson Collection.

The Crest Movie Theater on South Lumina Avenue began showing motion pictures in 1946. A popular destination for movies in the fifties and sixties, it was converted to a bar in the seventies where locals enjoyed their favorite bands. Today it is a fitness club. Note the poster for the Betty Davis movie. Courtesy of Star News.

capacity of 388, a balcony, and an orchestra seating arrangement. In the same year and across the street, the Bankhead's Neptune Restaurant opened, named for the god of the sea in Roman mythology. For years it was the town's only seafood house and regular visitors could conveniently get groceries at nearby Roberts and sundries at Newell's.

After the war, old social clubs prospered and new ones formed. In 1948 the Wilmington Light Infantry (WLI) Club celebrated its ninety-fifth anniversary with members whose ancestors fought for the Confederacy during the Civil War. The hotels and boarding houses and cottages were packed in the summer, as usual. It was 1946 when John Batson and Charlie Mills began

One of the many stages of Station One. This photo shows the tracks gone, before the sides were enclosed. Courtesy of the Wrightsville Beach Museum, Wayne Seal Collection.

Newell's in the early forties. To the left of Newell's is the information center, and the liquor store behind it with bars on the windows. Courtesy of the Wrightsville Beach Museum, Wayne Seal Collection.

Newell's in 1964. Courtesy of the Wrightsville Beach Museum, Wayne Seal Collection.

Patrons jam Newell's on a typical shopping day. Courtesy of the Wrightsville Beach Museum, Wayne Seal Collection.

The delightful, comfortable thirty-five room Pullen Cottage on the ocean at Wrightsville Beach. Circa 1950, courtesy of Bill Creasy.

Preparing for a day of skiing on Banks Channel are Albert Creasy and Peter Davis. *Circa 1950, courtesy of Bill Creasy.*

operation of the B & M Esso gas station on Harbor Island. Some locals can still remember "Pete," the resident red-winged black bird. For ten years, Pete migrated south and returned to the Esso station, apparently somewhat domesticated, much to the delight of those who frequented the gas station. The station operated (later under the name Exxon) until 1981.

The Newell's Store, a Wrightsville Beach retail institution for over fifty years, evolved from Lester Newell's drink stand and sandwich shop at Station One, the first trolley stop at the beach. Newell's evolved slowly into a general merchandise store where patrons could get staples, canned goods, fancy groceries, hardware items, gifts and novelties, toys, and wearing apparel. Newell's was probably one of the last places in the country where a customer could walk in and get a free cup of coffee. Cecil and Margaret Seal, who bought the business in 1976 from the Newell family, sold the business in 1992 to Wings, a retail chain.

Wrightsville Beach Lions' Club entertained State conventions in 1949 and 1952. An estimated crowd of 50,000 attended the 1952 convention, which was highlighted by an extravagant $1,000 aerial fireworks display. The women of Wrightsville Beach established domestic clubs during the social growth of the post-war years. The Dunes' Garden Club was organized in October of 1952 and the Home Demonstration Club was organized in October of 1960.

Wrightsville Beach School, constructed in 1955. *Photo by Beth Keane.*

The increase of permanent residents was evident in the development and growth of local churches and a school. Since Wrightsville was no longer a place of just summer homes, residents wanted an increase in fellowship with their neighbors and existing churches expanded while new ones were formed.

Wrightsville Methodist Church and congregation. Reverend Paul Browning, with (next to the three children) Alice Merkly, Dell White and Gladys Parker. Circa late fifties, courtesy of the Methodist Church.

Little Chapel on the Boardwalk in 1951.

Courtesy of the Little Chapel.

Saint Therese Catholic Church.

Photo by Greg Watkins.

Wrightsville Beach Baptist Church. *Photo by Greg Watkins.*

Wrightsville Marina on the Intracoastal Waterway in the early fifties. Note the old drawbridge in the distance. Courtesy of the North Carolina State Archives.

This aerial view shows Lumina in its expanded form with Crystal Pier Hotel and Restaurant to the right. Banks Channel condominiums have replaced the Pomander Walk Cottages in the foreground. Circa 1957. Courtesy of the Bill Creasy Collection.

This 1952 aerial photo shows the drawbridge, Intracoastal Waterway, Mott's Channel and Airlie Road. Courtesy of Bill Creasy.

The first service for the Wrightsville United Methodist Church was held on April 22, 1947. After several years of fundraising, ground breaking for the new church on Live Oak Drive took place in 1954. St. Mary's-by-the-Sea Catholic Church, the oldest church on Wrightsville Beach, dedicated a new brick church and rectory as Saint Therese in 1944. The current Sanctuary of the Little Chapel on the Boardwalk on North Lumina Avenue was completed in 1951, with the interior and exterior constructed of crabapple stone. The Wrightsville Beach Baptist Church was organized in 1954 as an outreach ministry of the Seagate Baptist Church of Wilmington. The original congregation consisted of thirty-nine charter members, and the church's first sanctuary was completed in 1955.

These churches continued to grow and build throughout the 1950's and 1960's.

With the increase in population, the need for a school arose. In 1953 construction began and the school opened later with three teachers, including Mr. John Bridgeman, the principal. Known as the "little school on the marsh",

Hurricane Hazel October 15, 1954, the greatest natural disaster and storm surge in North Carolina history. Eighteen feet above mean low tide at the exact time of the highest lunar tide of the year—the full moon. Winds at Wrightsville Beach were estimated at 125 mph with eight to ten inches of rain. Courtesy of the Wrightsville Beach Museum, Rajah Arab Collection.

The Waterway bridge. Courtesy of the Wrightsville Beach Museum, Dorathy H. Weathersbee Collection.

Airlie Road after Hurricane Hazel. Courtesy of the Wrightsville Beach Museum, Dorathy N. Weatherbee Collection.

Hazel damages. *From the Bill Creasy Collection.*

Augusta Street after Hurricane Hazel. Note the cottage washed into the center of the street.

Courtesy of the Cape Fear Museum.

Folder advertising Wrightsville Beach in the fifties. *Courtesy of the Wrightsville Beach Museum of History.*

Baseball fun on the beach in the fifties. Courtesy of the North Carolina State Archives and the Wrightsville Beach Museum.

Laughing with friends on the beach. *Courtesy of the Wrightsville Beach Museum, Billy Ulmer Collection.*

This family is rigged for a day of fishing. *Courtesy of the North Carolina State Archives.*

Lumina held a broad spectrum of events, including the Miss North Carolina Beauty Pageant. *Courtesy of the North Carolina State Archives.*

"Shuny" Brittain, former Wrightsville Beach life guard and minor league baseball player, opened a miniature golf course in 1956 that eventually expanded to include an arcade and amusement center. But "Shuny's" was not the first miniature golf course at Wrightsville. In 1930, locals had a chance to sharpen their putting skills at Lumina's miniature golf course.

From the Bill Creasy Collection.

it had ten classrooms, a library, and a combined cafeteria and auditorium.

As a new identity was forming for Wrightsville Beach, the community lost some of the businesses, buildings, and individuals which helped create it. In 1952 Tidewater Power Company merged with Carolina Power and Light Company. This consolidation marked the end of Tidewater Power Company, which had been such an influence on the early development of Wrightsville Beach. The following year Wrightsville lost one of its beloved local characters. William D. Polite "head waiter extraordinare" died in February, 1953. Mr. Polite worked for years at the Seashore Hotel and other hotels. He trained many waiters and waitresses, and at one time marketed his own cooking sauce.

The old two lane rolling bascule bridge kept the trolley track in place until it was dismantled in 1958. It was so well balanced that it could be hand cranked if the electric motor failed. The new drawbridge is in the background. From the Bill Creasy Collection.

Wrightsville Beach's first town hall is on the left, with the fire station flying the flag. Circa 1958, from the Bill Creasy Collection.

Wrightsville Marina in 1958.. Courtesy of Bill Creasy.

This photo from the fifties, shows the International Nickel Company saltwater testing plant. From the Bill Creasy Collection.

The estate of Pembroke Jones, circa 1954. *Courtesy of the New Hanover County Public Library.*

The caption of this classic pose was "Three Babes on the Beach." From left to right are Arlean Arwood, Ailene King, and Doris Barnes Ulmer. *Courtesy of the Wrightsville Beach Museum, Billy Ulmer Collection.*

In 1954 the nearby lodge of the former Pembroke Jones burned to the ground, marking the end of "the Golden Age."

Later in 1954, Wrightsville Beach suffered an upset still vivid in the minds of many older residents. Hurricane Hazel struck the coast of southeastern North Carolina at 10:42 a.m. October 15, 1954. Wrightsville experienced seas eight feet above normal high tide and wind gusts of one hundred forty miles per hour. Waynick Boulevard was flooded to a depth of several feet. Eighty-nine buildings were completely destroyed, one hundred fifty-six were badly damaged, and three hundred seventy-five were slightly damaged. One pier was damaged and one destroyed. The Beach suffered a total estimated loss of more than seven million dollars. Prominent damaged buildings included the Yacht Club, Ocean Terrace Hotel, and the Hanover Inn. Many homes and businesses were repaired or rebuilt, and many new enterprises were begun.

With a little promotion and a lot of great weather, Wrightsville Beach was soon back in full swing, with its sun, sand, fishing, competitions, and pageantry.

"Shuny" Brittain, former Wrightsville Beach life guard and minor league baseball player, opened a miniature golf course in 1956 that eventually expanded to include an arcade and amusement center. But "Shuny's" was not the first miniature golf course at Wrightsville. In 1930, locals had a chance to sharpen their putting skills at Lumina's miniature golf course.

In 1958 the old draw bridge was replaced with a bascule bridge design and named for Heide C. Trask. It was counterweighted so it could be

The Blockade Runner promised "Greater Popularity and Patronage" for southeastern North Carolina when it opened in the early sixties. *Courtesy of Bill Creasy.*

Johnnie Mercer's Pier has always been an attraction for the young and young at heart. **From the Bill Creasy Collection.**

Girls on Mercer's Pier in the early sixties. *Courtesy of Bill Creasy.*

The first surf movie came to the Crest at Wrightsville Beach on April 30, 1965. It was sponsored by the Onslow Bay Surf Club and Jack Hunt. *Courtesy of Robert Parker.*

Robert Parker makes a "Dropknee" turn at Columbia Street in June of 1966.

Photo by Charles Davis using one of the first water-resistant-housing instant Kodaks.

Jerry King waxes up before going out at the Stone Street jetty, September 1964.
Courtesy of Robert Parker.

raised and lowered easily every hour for sailboats and large vessels to travel on the Intracoastal Waterway.

The Blockade Runner Hotel was built in 1962 by Lawrence Lewis, Jr., a native of Wilmington. The Hotel and Convention Center promised to return Wrightsville Beach to its former position of eminence among Southern resorts. The local chamber of commerce promised that the hotel would be a tremendous credit to the entire state and would begin a new era in tourist attractions and resort trade for Wrightsville Beach and southeastern North Carolina.

Nayland Wilkins (on right) and Robert Parker (with surfboard on his head) leave Crystal Pier after a morning of surfing in the summer of 1965. *Courtesy of Robert Parker.*

In 1962, a branch of the First National Bank of eastern North Carolina opened on Wrightsville Beach, and later became known as Peoples Bank. That same year Mike Zezfellis purchased the Mira Mira Restaurant and Pier. He converted the large dining rooms into apartments, installed a small cafe on the ground floor, and changed the name to the Crystal Pier. The Bankhead sold out in 1962 to B. C. Hedgpeth, who renamed the restaurant "King Neptune."

The mid-sixties brought a renewed appreciation for the beach life, especially for teenagers and college students. It was the time of the Beach Boys music, and the surf was always up. In 1963 Robert Parker was one of the first on the beach to ride the modern fiberglass and foam surfboards. Robert and Hansen Surfboards of Candiff, California established the Onslow Bay surf team, the first on Wrightsville Beach. The other team members were Mike Curry, Mike Deep, Tommy Thompson, Joe Funderberg, Richard Verzaal, and Billy Curry. They competed on the East Coast from 1964 to 1966.

The town was booming and was attracting new business opportunities. In September 1965, Wrightsville Beach annexed Harbor Island. Construction began in 1967 on the Holiday Inn. Officially opened for business in 1969, the hotel provided much needed hotel space for the increasingly popular beach. In the late 1970s, ownership changed and the hotel

Redix Store opened in Wrightsville Beach in 1969. **Photo by Beth Keane.**

was renamed the Holoway Inn by the Sea. In the early eighties, it became a Sheraton Inn. In 1987, it reverted to a Holiday Inn. Due to the increasing popularity of Wrightsville Beach as a tourist destination, management decided to close the hotel for renovations in 1995 and the following year it reopened as the Holiday Inn Sunspree Resort, offering a full array of recreational facilities.

The Redix Store was established near the Intracoastal Waterway in August of 1969 by Mrs. D. D. Redick. Redix now serves as the community store, offering hardware, clothing, and sundries.

Lumina in later years still looked good in the autumn of its life. Circa 1958. Courtesy of Bill Creasy.

Four

The 70's, 80's, and 90's

The Town Municipal Complex, is surrounded by twenty acres of beautiful parks and landscaping. **Photo by Beth Keane.**

A S THE YEAR-ROUND POPULATION OF Wrightsville Beach burgeoned in the 1970s, it became necessary to expand the town's municipal facilities. After much negotiating by town officials, approximately twenty acres on Harbor Island was secured from the U.S. Department of Interior for $1.00. An experimental desalinization plant was renovated into office space for town officials, and a contract to construct a masonry fire station was awarded in 1971. Matching grants were used to develop the parks.

Fortunately, the small-but-beautiful downtown district of Wrightsville Beach and its modern era of architecture created in the forties and fifties endured the wrath of Mother Nature and the wrecking ball of progress. In the late sixties, seventies, and early eighties, Wrightsville Beach restaurants and bars were in their heyday, mostly in the downtown section but as far south as the Upper Deck at Lumina and as far north as the Palm Room and Sea Dog near Johnny Mercer's Pier. Some of the most popular were the Spot, the Crest's Rec Room, the Olympia, Hugo's, and the Wits End. Restaurants, boutiques, gift shops, and bars made for a variety of opportunities, but the charm of Wrightsville's history wasn't lost on the merchants. There developed a hot dog stand called "The Trolley Stop", a condominium called "Station One", and more recently, an ice cream parlor squeezed into an old trolley car.

In the seventies, height restrictions were a dominant theme of many conversations on the beach. The high rises were on the way. The Islander, Seapath Towers, and Station One forever changed the landscape of Wrightsville Beach. Not everyone was pleased with the new trend, and soon tighter restrictions were in place in an effort to keep the island from turning into wall-to-wall high rises.

The growth and change of Wrightsville Beach is symbolized by the community's most significant loss—the loss of Lumina. In August 1962, Relmon Robinson sold Lumina to Jake Lane, J. Lansing Smith, and Mike Vaughn. Lumina was not the popular spot it once was, and rumors spread that the new owners planned to renovate. The owners did not restore Lumina but did change its appearance and added a building called The Upper Deck. The Upper Deck sold beer and food and was popular with the then younger generation. In the mid-sixties Rock-n-Roll began to take over the dance floor of Lumina. Hall wrote, "A couple stands several feet apart and wriggles in any manner that the deafening sounds of Rock-n-Roll inspires them." Lumina Pavilion had provided an entertainment destination for residents and visitors for more than sixty years. The Pavilion's owners, after nine years of unsuccessful attempts to revive local interest in big band entertainment, saw the building condemned in 1971. Lumina's lights blazed for the last time in 1973, when in April, its 75-day demolition began. J. Lansing Smith said, "It was a fine place....it served its time."

As Wrightsville became a more popular tourist destination, large scale condominium complexes were planned in the early seventies. Billed as the "first high-rise ocean-front condominium apartment in the two Carolinas" the Islander, featuring sixty units, was built in 1973. Ten stories high, recreational facilities included an outdoor swimming pool, clubhouse, and tennis courts.

Memories of Lumina

We remember you now:
Your white with green trim and broad promenades of gray.
Shaded first floor with bath houses and refreshment stands,
And above a covered walk-way around the shiny dance floor,
Then the third, a balcony to watch the dancers do
The turkey-trot, the bunny-hug, the camel-walk,
Round trip for 35 cents on the electric cars and
Fine seafood at the Oceanic Hotel,
Crabbing and foot races on the beach and
The full moon behind the movie screen,
The five-cent streetcar to Newells' for a huge cone
and the way you stood strong against Hazel.
For the happiness and the light you brought our lives,
We remember you now.

Vicky Hodges Bellmann

Photo circa 1973 of Lumina, just before its demise. *From the Bill Creasy Collection.*

Right: **The Trolley Stop Hot Dog Stand, one of the most popular eating spots on the island in summer.** *Photo by Beth Keane.*

Then in 1976 Station One, named for the first trolley car stop on the beach, was completed. Erected by Venture Management of Atlanta, the building is eight stories high and six hundred feet long. This condominium project is ocean-front adjacent to the old Station One trolley stop at the corner of South Lumina Avenue and the Causeway.

The Trolley Stop Hot Dog Stand, located at old Station One on the trolley line, was opened by B. C. Hedgpeth in 1976. Several years later it was purchased by Ron and Winnie Krueger, who ran it until 1995. In April of that year, Jo Deane Combs and Kim Hall took over the beach's oldest and most popular hot dog stand. Along the Intracoastal Waterway, the Bridge Tender opened in 1976 as an upscale restaurant. A few years later and just a little south, the Dockside opened, with its focus on casual dining, simple but great food, and a splash of entertainment from time to time. Just north of these restaurants the drawbridge provides the only access to Harbor Island, from which two bridges connect to Wrightsville Beach. These bridges are used daily by the resident local population of 3,000. On big weekends in peak-season, the summer visitors and "day-trippers" swell the population to 50,000 per day.

The big issue in the eighties: development again. This time it was Shell Island. A thin ribbon of sand, marsh grasses, dunes, and local vegetation, once separated from Wrightsville Beach's north end by an inlet, was being developed. The inlet was filled in, the marsh was back-filled, docks built into the grasses, and the once separate barrier sand bar known as "Shell Island" is now a permanent part of Wrightsville Beach, connected with a paved road. Building consisted of huge condominium complexes, large homes, and a resort at the northern tip that was somewhat unlike the rest of the island. Groundbreaking

The Islander. *Courtesy of Beth Keane.*

Station One. *Courtesy of Beth Keane.*

Seapath Condominiums and Marina. Photo by Bob Blander.

took place in November 1985 for the 169-condominium structure made of concrete and steel called Shell Island Resort. The resort included a restaurant, pool, and fitness center with sauna.

Home-building began to reach new dimensions in the late eighties throughout the island. Overlooking the beach at 17 Ashville Street, the DeLaurentiss Cottage, built in 1986, is a monument to the presence of the film industry in Wilmington. Owned by the International

Miami Beach Spanish style. Courtesy of Beth Keane.

Film Corporation, the beach home encompasses approximately 4,000 square feet of floor area, with multiple decks and porches overlooking the ocean. The pink stucco Shell Island beach house located at 260l North Lumina Avenue is an example of "Miami Beach Spanish Style" architecture transplanted to Wrightsville Beach. This home was built in 1989 and has approximately 3,000 square feet. Many of the more recently constructed homes provide a complimentary blend of new designs with older forms, making the neighborhoods beautiful and interesting. The more sedate vacation cottages built at the turn of the century which still remain in many neighborhoods are gentle reminders of island life at its best.

Shell Island Resort Hotel. Courtesy of Beth Keane.

One of the attractions to Wrightsville Beach for visitors is something the residents have known for a long time. Over the years, we have developed some of the finest restaurants and seafood in the southeast. The Causeway Cafe, Clarence Fosters, Blockade Runner, Middle of the Island, Raw Bar, and Neptune are just a few. More recently and on a much larger scale, the Oceanic

Fireman killed in blaze at beach

■ Related story, photo, 1B

By Merton Vance
Staff Writer

WRIGHTSVILLE BEACH — The American flag at Wrightsville Beach Town Hall flew at half-mast Sunday while investigators searched the rubble of an oceanfront apartment for clues in a fire that killed volunteer fireman Robert M. Wynn and seriously injured another fightfighter early Sunday morning.

The fire broke out around 1:15 a.m. in the Doak Apartments at 551 S. Lumina Avenue. When firemen arrived, the building was engulfed and flames had spread to the adjacent Hanover Seaside Club.

A third building, the Carolina Temple Apartments, sustained minor damage. All three structures were unoccupied.

Two Wrightsville Beach volunteer firemen were trapped in the Seaside building by an explosion, which Fire Chief Everett Ward said was apparently caused by a liquified propane gas tank.

Fireman Wynn, 28, who died from his injuries, lived at 111 Owl Lane and was employed by the Blockade Runner Motor Hotel.

Fireman John Dennison, 21, was hospitalized with second degree burns over about 25 percent of his body. Dennison, who lives at 13 Island Drive, remained Sunday night at New Hanover Memorial Hospital.

Both firemen were taken to the hospital by rescue units from the New Hanover and Ogden Volunteer Rescue Squads, but Wynn could not be revived.

It was the first time in memory that a Wrightsville Beach fireman had been killed on duty, Ward said. He said the circumstances surrounding Wynn's death were still under investigation.

The death hit the fire department hard.

"It's something that takes you by surprise when it happens," Ward said.

Wrightsville Beach firemen carry injured comrade to safety early Sunday.

Photo by Raul Aizco

Wynn joined the fire department in August 1980. He had been seeking certification from the state community college system to teach firefighting courses, Ward said.

"He was very dedicated to learning and teaching fire practices," Ward said. "As a volunteer fireman, he gave of himself very unselfishly. He always exhibited a great deal of pride in what he was doing."

Wynn was born in Anderson, S.C. He is survived by his father, Carl Wynn, two sisters and a brother.

Funeral services will be at 2 p.m. Wednesday in the Robinson Funeral Home Chapel in Easley, S.C.

About 35 firefighters responded to the five-alarm blaze. The Wrightsville Beach Fire Department was assisted by units from Ogden, Winter Park and Seagate volunteer fire departments.

Firemen were able to save the Carolina Temple Apartments, just north of Doak Apartments. The south wall of that building was charred by flames.

Ward said firemen did not yet have a definite estimate on the amount of damage.

A brick chimney was about all that remained standing of the Doak Apartments. Only the front part of the Hanover Seaside Club, built in 1906, remained. A stiff, cold wind from the west-northwest spread flames quickly through the old wooden structures.

Some firemen were so close to the intense heat that the fronts of their helmets melted, Ward said.

The buildings were only about 15 feet apart, which made it easy for the fire to spread, Ward said.

The three story Doak Apartments building was owned by Rob-

ert R. and Betty Doak of Ralei and Charles W. and Irene Doak Rocky Mount.

The 500 block of Lumina Aven was closed by police during the fi and remained blocked to traffic day Sunday.

Investigators from the Wright ville Beach fire and police depa ments and the State Bureau of I vestigation began sifting throug the rubble Sunday, but were unab to determine the cause before dar Ward said investigators would r sume their probe today.

Left: **The Hanover Seaside Club burned in December 1981. Robert M. Wynn, for whom Wynn Plaza is named, died in the effort to control the blaze, which started in the Doak Apartments at 551 South Lumina Avenue. The article is from the Wilmington Morning Star and the photo is by Raul Aizcorbe.** *Courtesy of the Hanover Seaside Club.*

DeLaurentiss cottage. *Courtesy of Beth Keane.*

Right: **This home on the southern tip of Wrightsville Beach overlooks the ocean and Mason's Inlet.** *Courtesy of Nick Garrett.*

Aerial view of Shell Island. *Courtesy of the North Carolina State Archives.*

Restaurant replaced the old Crystal Pier Hotel (they kept the pier and spectacular view), which is close to the site of the famous Lumina Pavilion near the south end. Another popular spot, the Fish House, is perched on the Intracoastal Waterway and serves up sandwiches and seafood along with casual entertainment, and a great view. On the east side of the waterway, a restaurant called Wally's was constructed in the summer of 1990, and is one of the area's largest. The Sunday afternoon summer jam and dance sessions have become an institution at Wally's, attracting thousands to enjoy the sunset over the water with some reggae or Jimmy Buffet-style music. New owners in 1997 renamed it Pussers at Walley's.

Lumina Avenue, the street named after the site which in the past brought so much revelry to Wrightsville Beach, is also known for spots where people gather to socialize. The corner at Causeway and Lumina Avenue reflects the continual evolution of the beach's lifestyle by its changing landscape. Of all that lends Wrightsville Beach its special, small-town magic, Roberts Grocery is most typical. This family-owned business has changed sides of the street and grown over the years, but still retains the narrow aisles and friendly atmosphere that make even the first time visitor feel comfortable and at home. Roberts Market was started about 1919 by a Lebanese immigrant named Charles S. Robier, who was advised by his doctors to move south from New York for his respiratory condition. Locals had difficulty with the pronunciation of Robier, so he changed it to Roberts.

A short block south of Roberts' present location is Clarence Foster's, an upscale restaurant and bar with a sharp southwestern style. In the evening it is filled with young, khaki-clad professionals out for a night of fun, music, and spirits.

Oceanic Restaurant occupies the site of the old Crystal Pier Hotel, just to the south of where Lumina stood. It borrowed its name from the grand hotel that was over a mile further north, confusing some folks, but there's no confusion about its spectacular view or great food. Courtesy of the Oceanic Restaurant.

The Blockade Runner Beach Resort today.
With a restaurant, convention facilities, and
pool, it is the center of much of the social
activity at Wrightsville Beach in the nineties.
Courtesy of the Creative Resource.

Across the street, the King Neptune Bar and Restaurant usually draws a healthy crowd. The Hedgpeths sold the Neptune in 1987 to Bernard Carroll who upgraded the restaurant with an atmosphere of nostalgia, with pictures from the Twenties and Thirties on display. There's also a popular game where a brass ring is swung across the room to a hook on a post. It usually becomes more difficult (and interesting) as the evening progresses. Nearby is Reddogs, beach headquarters for ultra-cool surfers. Occasionally it has a quaint little drinking game: the beer is free until someone has to use the bathroom. Just north and on the west side of North Lumina Avenue is Buddy's, where the most laid-back of Wrightsville relax. The owner, Buddy Wiles, brought a little of Margaritaville back from Key West with him for this enterprise. Patrons enjoy oysters, crabs, cold beer, and a great juke-box. It could be Sloppy Joe's or Captain Tony's in Key West, but it is Buddy's at Wrightsville Beach.

Left Page and Above: **Roberts Groceries, then and now, a lesson in how some things never seem to change, and why they shouldn't. Operated for years by Eva and Bill Cross, it's a favorite spot to catch up on topics of local interest as well as to stock up on groceries.** *Older photo is from the mid-seventies, courtesy of Eva Cross. New photo was taken in 1997 by Greg Watkins.*

Reddogs, alias Sgodder's, alias Hugo's. *Photo by Beth Keane.*

King Neptune's. *Photo by Greg Watkins.*

About ten blocks north where Salisbury Street meets the ocean, is Johnnie Mercer's pier, where it seems time has stood still. The long soda fountain is reminiscent of the fifties, and a large game room stays packed with teenagers almost around the clock. A few doors away from Mercer's Pier is the Raw Bar, a favorite restaurant and pub for great seafood and onion hush puppies. It's a relaxed atmosphere where you can occasionally bump into a Hollywood celebrity taking a break from work on a local film.

Among the few structures that survived the fire of 1934, the Tar Heelia Inn on North Lumina Avenue with its sprawling, wrap-around porch is one of the oldest cottages on the beach, and the island's first locally-designated historic landmark. Built in 1910, this eight-bedroom boarding house was typical of its day, housing many locals and visitors and building quite a reputation for providing the best of the southern beach lifestyle. In 1990 its current owner purchased the house for restoration just in time to prevent its condemnation. The Inn has been highlighted in Southern Living magazine and from time to time been featured in local television shows. Occasionally hosting movie stars from the nearby studio, the house has retained the ambiance and flavor of years gone by. Sipping a mint julep while in one of the porch's twenty rockers or two hammocks is typical of today's activity. This house and its great history inspired the founding of the Wrightsville Beach Preservation Society.

The Society was begun in 1990, but without much success. Then one of the oldest and most beloved of Wrightsville Beach's institutions, Newell's, disappeared. A community landmark and town gathering place for fifty years was replaced almost overnight with a mega T-shirt shop called Wings.

Clarence Fosters (Old Mediterraneo's Restaurant and Bar.)
Photo by Greg Watkins.

Buddy's, outside and in. *Courtesy of Buddy Wiles.*

The restored 1910 Tar Heelia Inn. This cottage was the last lot on the North End extension for decades. Development stopped there because at the turn of the century, there was an inlet near the site of present-day Ashville Street. Photo by Greg Watkins.

This is one of the last photos of Newell's. The red sign is now part of a display called "The Stages of Station One" at the Wrightsville Beach Museum of History. From the Bill Creasy Collection.

Wings replaced Newell's at the site of Station One on the old trolley line. **Photo by Beth Keane.**

Wynn Plaza, the site of the old Municipal boat dock, was named for Robert M. Wynn, the only fireman at Wrightsville Beach to loose his life in the line of duty. The Wrightsville Beach Preservation Society uses the building to display vintage photos of the beach and enlighten everyone to the beach's rich history. The two vintage characters in the photo are Greg Watkins (left), founding Director of the Preservation Society and the Museum of History, and Bill Creasy, Preservation Society Historian and President in 1994. Courtesy of the *Wrightsville Beach Museum.*

Interest in the Preservation Society picked up as locals realized how fragile their few remaining historic landmarks were. Soon the Preservation Society convinced the town Board of Aldermen to let them display vintage photos of the beach at Wynn Plaza to help everyone appreciate Wrightsville's wonderful history. Interest in history and preservation grew, and in 1992 the town of Wrightsville Beach established its own Historic Landmark Commission consisting of five residents appointed by the board of aldermen to recognize and encourage the preservation of the few remaining landmarks on the beach.

As if to prove that history repeats itself, in 1992 another sperm whale washed ashore at Wrightsville Beach. This time it was a young whale, much smaller than "Trouble," the giant sperm whale that washed ashore in 1928. This one died unnecessarily because of ingesting debris and plastic.

In 1994 the Preservation Society, deciding to recreate some history of its own, established its annual historic celebration, "Lumina Daze," which is held each July during a full moon. A replica of the old

The Sperm whale that washed ashore north of Johnny Mercer's Pier in 1992. Photo by Greg Watkins.

Grant Hoover began printing the Wright Times magazine in 1994. The bi-monthly free publication keeps residents in the know and helps tourists find out what to do and where to do it. Courtesy of the Wright Times.

Lumina movie screen is built on the beach, silent movies or a Bogie and Bacall style film are shown, as the full moon rises over the ocean, and swing music from the 30's and 40's is danced to in the ballroom and on the patio of the Blockade Runner Beach Resort.

Another effort of the Preservation Society was to develop the Wrightsville Beach Museum of History. Fundraising for this effort took two years, and finally resulted in the moving and restoration of the 1907 historic Myers' Cottage landmark, the fourth-oldest cottage on the beach. The Museum opened in May of 1995 showing what life was like at the turn of the century on Wrightsville Beach. Exhibits include "Our beginnings as a barrier island," "Wrightsville and the Civil War," "Lumina the Lifestyle," and "Hurricane Hazel-the Big One." The permanent exhibits on display include a scale model of Wrightsville Beach circa 1910 complete with working trolley. The town leases the property to the Preservation Society which runs the Museum, located at 303 West Salisbury Street (near the volleyball courts). The Museum house is a splendid example of turn-of-the-century architecture at Wrightsville Beach.

Like the architectural and cultural evolution that has taken place at the beach, the natural evolution continues as well. As the beach cycles through its continuous process of erosion and rebuilding, the Army Corps of Engineers has begun a project to renourish it on a regular basis. A pipeline pumps sand from the bottom of the Banks Channel or an inlet, to the beach. In the eighties this was an every-five-year effort, and more recently seems to be more a function of funding than timing. As the island has become more developed through the years, the inlets have been filled in and built upon. The inlet that was once near Asheville Street ceased to exist in the twenties, and then the inlet at Salisbury Street was filled in, then the inlet near the location of the Holiday Inn was filled in. The long-term effect of the filling in of inlets and continuous

Museum on the move! Paul Pearsall, House Movers (Paul leading the way), crosses the bridge at Banks Channel. The town Board of Aldermen agreed to lease a corner of the town's twenty acres to the Preservation Society so the townspeople of Wrightsville Beach could have a museum. Courtesy of the Wrightsville Beach Museum.

Above: **The Lumina Daze Annual Historic Celebration began in 1994 and is held each July during a full moon. Events held during the celebration include a full moon swim in the ocean, classic movies shown on the beach, and swing music in the ball-room of the Blockade Runner Resort Hotel. Fred Astaire dance instructors give a demonstration in the photo.** *Courtesy of the Wrightsville Beach Museum.*

State of North Carolina

JAMES B. HUNT JR.
GOVERNOR

WRIGHTSVILLE BEACH PRESERVATION AWARENESS WEEK

1997

BY THE GOVERNOR OF THE STATE OF NORTH CAROLINA

A PROCLAMATION

WHEREAS, preservation is an important tool which can be used to safeguard history for future generations; and

WHEREAS, the Wrightsville Beach Preservation Society has furthered this aim by moving and renovating a 1908 beach house known as the Myers Cottage which serves as the Wrightsville Beach Museum of History; and

WHEREAS, the purpose of the museum is to capture the character of the town by educating the public to the days when travelers to Wrightsville Beach took the trolley to Lumina Pavilion where they danced to swing music and watched silent movies shown on a screen in the ocean; and

WHEREAS, the land, structures and lifestyle at Wrightsville Beach are vulnerable to natural elements such as wind, rain and water damage from hurricanes and coastal erosion from shifting sands in the inlets; and

WHEREAS, Wrightsville Beach Preservation Awareness Week will provide an opportunity to educate the public to ensure that this segment of our state's heritage is remembered for generations to come;

NOW, THEREFORE, I, JAMES B. HUNT JR., Governor of the State of North Carolina, do hereby proclaim July 20-26, 1997, as **"WRIGHTSVILLE BEACH PRESERVATION AWARENESS WEEK"** in North Carolina, to facilitate greater awareness of Wrightsville Beach's historic preservation.

JAMES B. HUNT JR.

IN WITNESS WHEREOF, I have hereunto set my hand and affixed the Great Seal of the State of North Carolina at the Capitol in Raleigh this thirtieth day of May in the year of our Lord nineteen hundred and ninety-seven, and of the Independence of the United States of America the two hundred and twentieth.

Lumina Daze Historic Celebration activities, clockwise from top left: the Fred Astaire dancers jazz up the swing music in the ballroom; classic movies are shown on the beach under the moonlight, Choral Robert's Quartet harmonizing; Monique Wright and Jim Greiner strike a pose; the Sweet Adelines arrive at Lumina in grand style; and early 1900's beach attire sported by Nancy Faye Craig, Greg Watkins, and Melody Evans.

Retaining turn-of-the-century charm, the Winniford Shepard Morrison Cottage is still located on South Lumina Avenue. Photo by Beth Keane.

*The Wise Cottage is a beautiful example of the large cottages that still add their character to Wrightsville Beach. **Photo by Greg Watkins.***

The Carolina Yacht Club in the nineties. *Photo by Beth Keane.*

dredging has unpredictable effects on erosion. Preserving the "Playground of the South" requires millions of dollars to replenish the strand with sand lost to erosion from the changing hydraulics of the inlets and the Atlantic ocean. Renourishment debates are now as constant as the erosion, ranging from cost and inconvenience to concerns about the environment and tourism. In October 1993 the question "Where's the Beach?" was often asked about the northern tip of Shell Island which was said to be "eroding at a fast rate." The Wrightsville Beach Board of Aldermen asked the Army Corps of Engineers to study the problem. As of this publication, the Atlantic Ocean was winning this contest.

As if normal erosion were not enough, in 1996 Mother Nature hit North Carolina with two hurricanes. Both Bertha and Fran took dead aim at

Dredge barge used for renourishment on the beach. *From the Bill Creasy Collection.*

Residents are treated to many of natures surprises. These two waterspouts appeared early one morning in the spring of 1995 at the end of Augusta Street. Photo by Greg Watkins.

Hurricanes Bertha and Fran made 1996 a year many residents in Wrightsville Beach would like to forget.

Left Page: **Raleigh Street damages.** Photo by Greg Watkins.

Below: **Destruction on North Lumina.** Photo by Greg Watkins.

Wrightsville Beach with bulls-eye accuracy. Bertha at 9:00 p.m. on July 12th resulted in the loss of seventy-five feet of Johnnie Mercer's Pier, widespread damage to roofs and piers, damage to about one hundred twenty-five homes (about $712,000), and severe erosion to Mason Inlet near Shell Island Resort. Fran arrived at 11:00 p.m. on September 5th. Fran's ninety-eight mile per hour winds and twelve-foot storm surge caused $20.5 million in residential damages, destroyed thirteen houses, damaged five hundred sixty-two others, and resulted in a cleanup cost around $197,000.00. For those who could remember, memories of Hurricane Hazel in 1954 came flooding back. Again, the residents of Wrightsville Beach rebuilt, and in less than a year's time, life was back to normal.

Each Memorial Day, Fourth of July, and Labor Day, Wrightsville Beach is forced to deal with another dilemma: not a single parking space can be found on the island. With fifty thousand visitors arriving each day on big summer weekends, and only two thousand parking spaces, finding an empty spot is like finding a needle in a haystack. The local residents try and do their shopping and errands before the traffic comes to a near standstill on the beautiful but crowded summer days.

In the spring Wrightsville Beach hosts the Cape Fear Marlin Tournament, fast becoming one of the best fishing tournaments on the East Coast. In September approximately two hundred fifty boats participate in the annual Wrightsville Beach King Mackerel Tournament, resulting in thousands of pounds of king mackerel being weighed in on the docks.

Each summer, one of the biggest parties of the year takes place at the annual Lumina Daze Historic Celebration. It is held each year during a full moon at the Blockade Runner Beach Resort Hotel. This event draws thousands and features swing music from the thirties and forties, moonlight swimming, and vintage movies (sometimes silent) shown on a movie screen built on the

The modern Wrightsville Beach is a beautiful blend of the old and the new. This aerial view shows the draw bridge in the lower left. Wally's is the large white-roofed building in the center on the Intracoastal Waterway.

Postcard from the Bill Creasy Collection. Photo circa 1996 by Jim Doane.

In the summer, parking spots are hard to find. Photo by Greg Watkins.

Right Page: **Wrightsville Beach is as crowded as ever. This photo was taken from Johnny Mercer's Pier on Memorial Day weekend in 1997. Courtesy of Greg Watkins.**

beach. Old slides are shown and vintage photos are on display. This fund raiser for the non-profit Preservation Society is one of the most festive events of the year.

Another rapidly-growing event is the annual Holiday Flotilla in November. The parade of boats of all shapes and sizes cruise at night through Mott's Channel and Banks Channel, all clad in Christmas lights. Judging takes place at a reviewing stand in front of the Blockade Runner Hotel. Over fifty boats have participated in the event, which is followed by a spectacular display of fireworks. Afterwards, a beachwide celebration takes place.

Wrightsville Beach today is as crowded and vibrant as anytime in its past. Each summer ever-greater numbers of tourists come from all over the country to enjoy its unique character, charm, and friendly residents. Each fall, as the tourists begin to depart, the locals "reclaim" their island for themselves, and fall, winter, and spring have become their favorite seasons.

Growth and development on Wrightsville Beach have almost reached capacity. The difficult task ahead for residents and visitors is to resist the natural tendency to develop more densely, and to preserve what remains of our island's special charm, character, and history.

One of the supporters of the Wrightsville Beach Preservation Society is Chris Bellamy, a popular singer of local folklore, who writes in his "Lumina Lights" song:

"Now most times summers are crowded,
and people are everywhere,
and condos stand by a restaurant,
where Lumina used to be,
But sometimes late in the evening,
when I go for a walk by the sea,
I can still feel the magic and romance,
of Lumina here by the sea."

Chris Bellamy sings a tune on the porch of the Wrightsville Beach Museum.
Photo by Greg Watkins.

Main Street (North Lumina Avenue) looking south from Columbia Street in 1958. Crest Movie Theater is on the left, followed by the hardware and bake store and the Angus Bull Steakhouse (where Roberts Groceries is now). Further down the street on the left are the Washerette and Spot Bar (where Clarence Foster's is now). Just past those buildings on the left was Sly's Bingo and the Wit's End Bar (where Sweetwaters is today). Courtesy of Bill Creasy.

November fireworks during the Holiday Flotilla. *Photo by Patrick Pitzer.*

Boats reflecting at night during the Holiday Flotilla in Banks Channel. *Photo by Patrick Pitzer.*

Left and Right Page: **Aerial views of Wrightsville from the south and north ends. Photos April 1997.**

Courtesy of the Creative Resource.

Surfers still enjoy the ride. *Photo by Patrick Pitzer.*

Left and Above: **The serenity of Wrightsville Beach is appreciated by all of its residents.** *Photos by Patrick Pitzer.*

Left: **A baby Loggerhead turtle makes its way to the ocean.** *Courtesy of the Wrightsville Beach Turtle Watch program. Photo of turtle tracks courtesy of Greg Watkins.*

Moon over Harbor Island. *Photo by Greg Watkins.*

Sunrise. *Photo by Patrick Pitzer.*

Museum in place. Built entirely through volunteer efforts and private financing, the Wrightsville Beach Museum is a good example of community cooperation between citizens and local businesses. Photo by Linda Caden.

Sunrise at Mercer's pier. The future looks bright for Wrightsville Beach as it prepares to celebrate its first one hundred years as an incorporated town. Photo by Greg Watkins.

Index

orn and raised in Bethesda, Maryland, Greg graduated with a Bachelor of Science degree in Business Administration from the University of Maryland. After working for IBM in Washington, D.C., he moved to North Carolina where he became a general contractor in Raleigh and Benson. Greg moved to Wrightsville Beach and several years later bought and restored the Tar Heelia Inn and retired. The Inn and its history motivated Greg to found the Wrightsville Beach Preservation Society. He was appointed by the Town Board of Aldermen to the Wrightsville Beach Historic Landmark Commission, and served as its first commissioner for two years. In 1994 Greg established the first annual Lumina Daze Historic Celebration for the Preservation Society and as founding director of the Wrightsville Beach Museum of History, opened its doors to the public in 1996. This book is the latest of his efforts to preserve the character and charm of the island he calls home.

DISCOVER

READ

EXPLORE

LEARN

**NEW HANOVER COUNTY
PUBLIC LIBRARY**

If found, please return to:
201 Chestnut St.
Wilmington, NC 28401
(910) 798-6300
http://www.nholibrary.org